TASK-CEN▯   ▯K

To Jan and Annie

Task-Centred Social Work

MARK DOEL
PETER MARSH

ASHGATE

© Mark Doel and Peter Marsh 1992

Published by
Ashgate Publishing Limited
Gower House
Croft Road
Aldershot
Hants GU11 3HR
England

Ashgate Publishing Company
Suite 420
101 Cherry Street
Burlington, VT 05401-4405
USA

Ashgate website: http://www.ashgate.com

British Library Cataloguing in Publication Data
Doel, Mark
    Task-centred social work.
    I. Title   II. Marsh, Peter, *1950-*
    361.32

Library of Congress Cataloging-in-Publication Data
Doel, Mark
    Task-centered social work / Mark Doel, Peter Marsh.
    p. cm.
    Includes bibliographical references and index.
    1.Task-centered social work. I. Marsh, Peter E.   II. Title.
HV40.D63   1992
361.3'2–dc20   91-32769
                                                        CIP

Reprinted 1998, 2000, 2002, 2003, 2004, 2008

ISBN 978 1 85742 070 8 (pbk)

Phototypeset by Intype, London
Printed and bound in Great Britain by MPG Books Ltd, Bodmin, Cornwall

Contents

The model
Recording in task-centred social work
The written agreement – case example

Acknowledgements

We would like to record our grateful thanks to our colleagues and trainees on task-centred projects and training programmes. Many trainees in different agencies and on qualifying programmes have helped us learn more about the model. We would particulary like to thank Sue Roberts and Catherine Sawdon for their help and support in establishing training programmes in task-centred practice in their respective Social Services Departments. Recently, the Social Work in Partnership project has enabled us to explore task-centred work in a number of new ways and Mike Fisher, Bill Reid and Clive Newton have helped us think carefully about the task-centred model. But over all the period that we have been developing this work the help, support and skilled work of Celia Atherton, Nano McCaughan, Jenny Stoker and Anne Vickery have been particularly important to us. We acknowledge an important debt to them.

Introduction

Contemporary social work practice is generally shrouded from professional and public view. Workers have few, if any, methods for learning from the successful or unsuccessful practice of others. Clients rarely participate in an informed choice of the service that they might obtain, not least because succinct descriptions of practice, with some analysis of outcome, are rarely available and so cannot be shared. Social work is very far from logging the experiences of practice and then developing practice on the basis of worker and client views, and the outcome of particular approaches. Apart from the law, the main guide to practice seems to be agency routine, professional folklore and personal foible. Each encounter is lost to the individual worker and to others because it is not entered into the pool of knowledge and experience.

To people outside of social work this must seem a surprising state of affairs. Why isn't practice developing by building on the most successful work? Why aren't clients contributing directly to this development? Some social workers may answer that the demands of day-to-day practice are often overwhelming, leaving little space to analyse the factors which lead to success or failure and even less to log those factors in a systematic fashion.

Lack of time is only one factor. In addition, the profession has lacked common frameworks to catalogue its achievements and its failures. How do social workers talk to each other about the outcomes of their work? In some professions we might look to the customers to force the pace, but social work's customers rarely have the opportunity to get together to compare notes.

Finding out what works is not easy in social work. It stands at a complex junction where very small and very large forces are at play; making judgements about what helped and what hindered is as much art as science. However, the willingness to ask the question, *what works?* is as important as the possibility of answering it. And there are some answers available.

If we cannot or will not discuss questions like *what works?* how can we ask users of the services to trust us? For example, a parent of a school child wants to talk with the teacher about *what works* for his or her child. Some parents will be interested in all aspects of their child's development, others might emphasize academic attainment, social progress or sporting achievements. The parent looks to the teacher for a professional understanding of what promotes children's development in general and their own child's in particular. This builds trust on the basis of mutual understanding – not on ignorance or unquestioning faith.

Social workers need the tools to be able to discuss *what works* or, at least, what *might* work and to discuss this not just with each other, but also with the users of social work. This requires a model of practice which will bring system to the experiences of practitioners.

In addition to a notion of good practice, there is another reason why it is important to help social workers to communicate with each other and with their clients about what they do and whether it works. That factor is the rapid change in the nature of the social work job brought about by major legislation affecting the probation service and the social services. Twenty years after Brewer and Lait (1980) wrote their apocalyptic diatribe, *Can Social Work Survive?*, we can see that although social work may survive, the social work task could be balkanized.

The potential for fragmentation is increased by the deepening divide between issues of care and control in social work. As the voluntary functions in social work attract the interests of the private sector, the unattractive supervisory functions could become marginalized as part of a diminished state social work service. It is crucial that we avoid a two-tier service.

All of this makes our task in this book urgent. We need to develop an understanding of what a model of practice is and a working knowledge of specific models. In this way practitioners can begin to compare notes about what works, when and with whom. They can begin to research their own practice and to involve the users of the social services in this process. Together they can speak with authority about the value of social work.

We have written this book in order to provide an introduction to a systematic model of practice. It is a model with an explicit ethical base and a practical application which has been well-researched. It is this research pedigree which attracts us to task-centred practice, one of the few models of practice that is home-grown within social work, and one which has been tried and tested in virtually every social work setting.

Task-Centred Social Work provides both a broad framework and a detailed practice guide which bridges the care and control divide. It continually guides the worker and the client towards asking and answering the question *what works?* and it provides a structure which enables comparisons to be made between that work then and this work now, that work there and this work here.

The task-centred model promotes a partnership between the workers and the user of the service, and makes it clear when this partnership is not possible to achieve. It also makes explicit issues of power in social work relationships and, as Coulshed (1988, p. 55) writes, 'the task-centred approach is the one most favoured by those who are trying to devise models for ethnic-sensitive practice'. By confronting issues of power directly and by coming clean about the use of professional authority, in a modest way it promotes anti-oppressive practice.

A guide to this book

We hope to put forward the main elements of the task-centred model in a clear and logical manner. First and foremost, this book is written with an intention that the material in it can be put to *use*. The book's structure follows the different stages of the model, from the first contact with a potential client through to the ending of the work. We think that this approach working in sequence through the stages that a practitioner would follow, provides the best framework for understanding the model. The penalty of such an approach is that the overall shape of the model cannot be seen clearly until the end, though the outline contained in this introduction may help. We shall briefly describe the model and the link with the relevant chapters.

The model

How is task-centred practice carried out? Primarily, by an active intervention with an emphasis on the role of the client in negotiating and undertaking appropriate programmes of help. It is a doing model, where learning will be as likely to occur by demonstration as by discussion. It is a participative model, where the client should be as fully informed and as fully involved as possible. The work will be based on an *agreement between the worker and the client* which will cover the problems to be addressed and the goals to be achieved. When necessary, these problems and goals will include those specified by legislative duties or by a court. This agreement, which will necessarily be based upon negotiation, starts the work in a participative style.

Chapter 2 outlines the ways that a mandate for intervention may be established and how this important issue is addressed in task-centred practice, and Chapters 3 and 4 explain the ways in which this mandate is carried out in practice by the exploration of problems, the clarification of goals and the use of written agreements.

Once the basis for work is established, the worker and the client proceed in a series of incremental steps towards the goals. This work is subject to regular review. The incremental steps will involve the client and the worker undertaking tasks in order to reach the agreed goals, and these tasks may themselves involve collaboration with other people. The worker may need to help the client carry out certain tasks by advice, encouragement or skill training. The regular review highlights the progress of work and pinpoints any need to address different problems or revise goals. Chapter 5 describes the details of the work on tasks which is central to the model, and Chapter 6 outlines the review and ending of an intervention.

In summary, the pattern of the work is a movement from *problems* through a sequence of *tasks* to *goals*. This is a progression from something which is wrong (problems) to something which is wanted (goals). Problems and goals are both agreed in the initial stage and the movement occurs by the undertaking of a number of actions (tasks). Tasks are effective because they are part of an overall action plan; any one task is unlikely to lead directly to the goal. Clearly, there are strong parallels with the way that we tackle significant problems in our lives; we try to work out what is wrong, we try to see what is wanted in the light of this and we take a number of steps which we hope will move us towards what is wanted.

In task-centred practice the worker and the client will agree at the outset how long the movement from problems to goals is likely to take. In general the *time limit* will be as short as reasonably possible. If it is likely to exceed about three months, or if there is a reason for long-term involvement (such as a statutory order), work can proceed by a series of shorter-term agreements.

All of these ingredients will appear familiar to social work practitioners. They follow themes that feature in most practice and, at a general level, they would be subscribed to by many social workers who do not claim to be using this approach. However, in our experience there is often a chasm between an agreement with general themes and an ability to put these into detailed practice. This book aims to bridge that divide and to explore (in Chapter 7) some common misconceptions about task-centred practice.

The structure of the chapters

In order to illustrate the model in action we have provided a Case Example. This concludes each chapter from 2 to 6, taking the reader from one stage to the next with the same case. Inevitably, one example is limiting, but it is carefully chosen to help to outline the model; of course, it cannot represent all of task-centred practice.

We have also decided to provide examples from everyday life throughout the book in order to illustrate the link between the model of problem-solving in task-centred work and the models that we might apply in our own lives. This makes an important link between the situations faced by users of social services and those faced by all citizens. We all have problems of one sort or another – there is not one world of problems for clients and another for professionals. This is an important principle, though we recognize that the problem examples in this book are not so pressing as those experienced by many clients; the examples are designed solely as *illustrations* of the process of problem-solving.

A basic handbook

We hope that the book will be used as a practice handbook and we have included a number of checklists (Appendix 1) which beginners may use to assess their own practice, or a supervisor or teacher to help others. The book is introductory and there is a brief guide to further reading to help establish a good basis for practising task-centred work (Appendix 2). The limits on an introductory book are evident; for example, we have not been able to cover specific settings such as probation or group care, nor have we addressed task-centred groupwork and the latest developments in task-centred family work. The reader will need to move to more specialized literature to cover these areas.

Getting started

Task-centred work is a demanding discipline. The skills and knowledge needed are as complex as any in social work and they rest on a commitment by the practitioner to provide a service which is based on the twin principles of openness and research-minded practice. Without these principles, task-centred practice will be enacted as a parody; with these principles it is an important key for both worker and client to unlock the question, *what works?*

1 A Practice Model

Over the past 30 years there has been a steady growth in the development of task-centred practice. It is a model of practice that originates within social work itself and that has been developed by social workers and social work researchers. The authors of this book have followed in that tradition, basing their work on many years' experience of using the model, and also on the training and research they have undertaken in task-centred work.

Evaluating a practice model

Why should we be paying attention to task-centred practice? There are three reasons why a model of practice may be considered worthy of our detailed attention; there are ethical reasons why we might want to criticize or adopt certain approaches, there are research reasons and there are practical reasons.

Ethics

Social work has always been concerned with ethical dilemmas, not least because of an active involvement with individuals and families in society's marginal groups. Social workers regularly work with people who are stigmatized or discriminated against. The value placed on human attributes, for instance being able-bodied or young or white, will often feature in the options that people have in society and the ways that social workers can help people to maximize those options. Questions about the intrinsic worth of different human attributes will inevitably be high on the social work agenda. At the most general level this has been expressed in the Codes of Ethics that social work organizations have adopted. The International Federation of Social Workers (1976), for example, begins its code with 'Every human being has a unique value' – an expression of the way that social work has always attempted to emphasize the dignity and worth of *all* members of society. But ethical questions in social work are not just about the value of all members of society, they are also about the rights that individuals and groups have to be treated fairly when they are subject to social intervention in their lives (BASW, 1980; Watson, 1985). These questions are particularly prominent when the liberty of people is at stake. Social workers have been given powers to be involved in the removal of children from their parents, the supervision of offenders in the community, and the compulsory treatment of mental ill-health. Social workers involved in these processes will always be concerned to see that they have acted in a way that is morally defensible.

Part of any judgement about the worth of a practice model must be the way that it fits the ethical concerns of social work practice.

Research

Alongside consideration of the way that ethical issues feature within a practice model there needs to be a judgement made concerning its effectiveness (Wood, 1978; Thomlinson, 1984; Reid and Hanrahan, 1981, 1982). Given the kind of problems that are being dealt with, does the model help resolve them? Questions of efficiency also need to be addressed: if the problems are solved is this the only way of solving them, and if there are alternatives are those alternatives quicker and simpler, or slower and more complex? Effectiveness and efficiency can be explored by research evaluations of practice involving a scientific consideration of the model.

Part of the judgement of a model is therefore a research judgement, but this area is not one that can be divorced from ethical considerations. There may, for example, be very effective means of problem-solving that should be regarded as ethically unacceptable.

Practicality

The final judgement concerns the practical application of a model. Some approaches may be ethically acceptable as well as effective and efficient (within the current limits of knowledge) but they may also be extremely hard to put into practice in the real world of social work. There are constraints on practice that come from the resources available to practitioners who may not have appropriate equipment or facilities. There are constraints on practice because of the ways that clients are able to respond to the requirements of a practice model, perhaps being unable to keep to a particular programme schedule. There are constraints on practitioners because of the actions and styles of organizations and institutions that they have to deal with, in the form of both explicit and implicit policies and procedures. Practice development must take place in this practical context (see for example, Reid and Epstein, 1972, Chapter 11).

The practicality of the approach, in common with the previous two issues, does not stand alone as a reason for adoption of a model. No one would suggest that practicality should over-rule ethical and scientific considerations: it should be considered alongside them.

Evaluating the task-centred model

What are the key concepts within task-centred practice that will enable us to make a judgement under the three headings of ethical, research and practical concerns?

Ethics

The client's views are at the centre of task-centred practice. Good task-centred work must focus in detail on the client's views and clients must be aware that their views have been carefully explored. There will be occasions when those views cannot be acted on, for example if they suggest impractical actions, and there will be times when those views will need to be thoroughly discussed, for example if the views suggest actions which directly affect other people. Listening carefully does not mean agreeing. There are many occasions when we feel that we have been heard, 'we have had our say', but at the end of the day the person that we are talking to does not agree with us.

How do we judge whether or not we 'have had our say'? At the most basic level we will need the time to make the points we would like to make, but we also need to see evidence from the listener that they know what we mean, for example by the listener paraphrasing back to us the viewpoint that we have expressed (Epstein, 1985). We might also want to judge the level of interest given to our view by the way that any final decision addresses that view; for example by re-stating the view as a form of preface to any decision that is made and then stating the reasons that it is or is not incorporated into the particular decisions. The space to express the view, the way that it is received and the way that any action relates to it are all important elements of our judgement about 'having our say'. Task-centred practice emphasizes all these factors as key parts of the practice model (Fortune, 1981). These factors are important in task-centred work not just because they are decent parts of human interaction (although the importance of that should not be undervalued) but because they are central to a principled stance that is taken within the model that the work should be *open* to challenge from the client, and from others who may be involved in judging practice. Task-centred work is, fundamentally, an *open* model of practice.

The openness of the model allows the client and others the opportunity of challenging the work undertaken. What opportunity for challenge or discussion do we expect in the services that we receive? At a basic level we usually expect access to the people providing the service. But these discussions are one-sided if the service itself is not clear to the recipient. If you are discussing your child's progress with a teacher, it is difficult to know what to make of slow progress in reading if you do not know the methods for teaching reading, the reasons why those methods are used, and the ways that those methods are enacted at the school. You need to know something about the service itself in order to discuss it properly; this means a reasonable level of detail of the purpose, principles and the alternatives. Having access to the person giving the service and knowing something about the service allows the person receiving it to call to account the person who is giving it (NCVO, 1984). An open service should be an accountable service and task-centred practice deliberately aims to be as accountable as possible to the client.

It is important to be clear that the term *accountable* is being used here in the literal sense of *giving an account*. The worker will be accountable to various people and to organizations and institutionalized procedures during different parts of the work. Task-centred work does not affect this (although as we shall argue later it does accommodate these different elements very well). The principle that any task-centred practitioner will follow is that the client is owed an account alongside other elements of accountability.

What is the effect of this principled stance on offering an account? It makes two major contributions to practice – a contribution towards the empowerment of clients and a contribution towards anti-oppressive practice. The contribution is primarily about making issues of power and oppression as clear as possible. Many social work decisions are linked to questions of values and ethics (Rhodes, 1986), and the notion of being able to give an account of decisions and actions allows those ethical issues to be assessed by the client. It can make prejudice, or the lack of it, more evident. The emphasis on open practice in task-centred work highlights the ethical nature of so much of the work and, by making clear the practitioners'·and the agencies/institutions' values, it offers the client and others the chance to participate in questioning or supporting those values. Task-centred practice should make it evident when the values contribute to discrimination or are based on racism or sexism. As we shall explore further in Chapter 2 the values underlying decisions and actions need to be clear and explicit in good task-centred practice.

Of course task-centred work with individuals is insufficient to challenge discrimination and to provide anti-oppressive services. There is no direct impact on access to the services, or on issues of an interpersonal nature such as differences in ethnicity or gender between worker and client. These and other issues need to be addressed so that we may provide the best service to all citizens. In its principled stance on open and accountable practice, task-centred work is an important element in the overall development of genuinely anti-discriminatory services.

Research

From its earliest days research has underpinned task-centred practice. The model's origins lie in research (Reid, 1963; Reid and Shyne, 1969) and a continuing flow of studies have developed the work over the years (see for example, Reid and Epstein, 1972; Goldberg et al., 1977; Butler et al., 1978; Goldberg et al., 1984; Reid, 1978, 1985; Fortune, 1985a; Rooney, 1988b). There is also a substantial literature of useful research techniques for model development (see for example, Reid, 1987a; Wodarski et al., 1982; Davis and Reid, 1988; Rooney, 1988b; Benbenishty, 1989). Research is central to task-centred practice.

What is particular to the task-centred research base? First and foremost it is the emphasis that is put on the research endeavour as a key component of practice development (Marsh, 1986; Ivanoff et al., 1987). Research is not an optional extra in task-centred work. It is, alongside openness, at the heart of the model. Skilled task-centred practitioners will be thinking in a *research-minded* fashion as they engage in the work. They will expect the research literature to inform their practice; for example, in Chapter 5 we discuss the research reasons for the use of a particular sequence of activities when developing tasks. Task-centred practitioners will also expect to contribute to the research; for example, seeing if the work they undertake on a particular problem area is consistently more successful if done in one way rather than another.

The second element of the task-centred research base is that it spans the complete range of social work settings – from hospitals to homes for elderly people, from work with couples to work with groups, from probation to child care. There is now material within the task-centred research tradition in all major social work settings (see Appendix 2). This is not a model of practice that is solely tested on one client group, nor is it a model that is primarily based on studies conducted outside of social work.

The third element of the research base is the emphasis that it gives to the *limits* of knowledge and the *limits* of actions within task-centred work. Because research plays such an important role in the model, a task-centred practitioner will be fully aware that there are still many answers to be found to the practice questions faced within social work. There is both an authority within a research-based model and a humility. You know what you don't know, and that is an important element of good practice. Research into social work intervention has often shown that there are minimal gains from the work undertaken, and that the effects of intervention can indeed be perverse, with clients that receive the service actually doing worse than those who do not (Grey and Dermody, 1972; Fisher, 1973; Sheldon, 1986). These results must be taken seriously, although we must also recognize that the nature of many social interventions is very complex and, as Joel Fischer (1978) has noted in 'Does anything work?', the results of social interventions other than social work are not that bright either. Research brings this humility into the centre of task-centred practice. Task-centred workers should be aware of what is going into the intervention (input), and of what the results are (output) in the context of the limits of current knowledge.

Task-centred work sits comfortably within the wider research efforts within social work. Research into outcomes has shown that social work should concentrate its development work on practice models that work within time-limited periods, that focus their change efforts clearly and that undertake joint work between worker and client (Reid and Hanrahan, 1982). Task-centred work falls into this category. In addition the research on task-centred work itself has shown, for example, that it is a popular way of working (Gibbons et al., 1979), that it produces better problem-solving than 'supportive attention' on its own (Reid, 1978), and that the results of its short-term approach are at least equivalent to long-term approaches (Reid and Shyne, 1969). This, and the other research into task-centred work, is a sound basis for the model but the real strength lies in the value given to the research approach itself. Building a social work model on the basis of careful assessment and evidence should provide important safeguards for the client and a sound foundation for practice.

Practicality

There is little value to an open and research-based model if the components of that model cannot be practised in the real world of social work. The tasks that workers undertake, the clients that they see, and the resources that are available must all be taken into account when we assess the relevance of a practice model. How does task-centred work measure up in this respect?

There is a tendency in social work writing for The Grand Statement (for example, 'social workers should combat this or that aspect of racism/sexism etc.') unaccompanied by much in the way of practical advice. This tendency may be related to a number of factors, ranging from slipshod thinking to the fact that many academics and senior figures in the field do not have current practice experience. Whatever the origins of the problem, it does raise significant difficulties for social workers who need a technology attached to any advice or development that is proposed. It is quite reasonable to say 'that's all very well, but how do we do that in the real world of practice?' Task-centred work offers such a technology. There are clear and practical examples in the literature and the overall development of the model is undertaken by the detailed development of practice tools and techniques. Moreover task-centred work has been developed within social work itself and tested in a wide variety of circumstances. It has a good pedigree for being both practical and relevant.

Social work itself is made up of a number of different jobs and any practice model must be clear which of the jobs it addresses. In particular there are jobs which emphasize the care aspects of the work and jobs which emphasize the control aspects (Day, 1981). Social work writing has not found it easy to span the twin elements of care and control. However the reality of practice is that it is usually an *emphasis* on either care or control, not a rigid demarcation, and practice models need to handle both aspects of the work. Task-centred work is designed to do just that, showing as clearly as possible the elements of the work based primarily on care and those based primarily on control.

Finally, we should emphasize that the practicality of a model also needs to be judged by client views (Maluccio, 1979; Fisher, 1983; Marsh, 1983; Sainsbury, 1983; Shaw, 1984; NISW, 1988), or perhaps this is better phrased as judging it by the level to which it pays attention to the client's view of its attractiveness. Clients deserve as attractive a service as possible, perhaps particularly so in circumstances where they are likely to have little option about receiving some sort of service (Booth, 1983; NISW, 1988) because of lack of alternative or because of court decisions. Providing as popular a service as possible must be one of the considerations in the choice of practice model.

All models have a number of practical limits and the two main ones within task-centred work probably apply to all of the practice models that are currently under development. First, its technology seems to be unsuitable to situations where families are in constant crisis. The emphasis on planning, albeit in time-limited periods, is very difficult to maintain in the face of new problems occurring in short periods of time and a reactive style of practice probably has to be adopted in these circumstances. Secondly, there are some situations where a worker needs to work with a client who does not accept the right of the practitioner to intervene at all, having no desire for that intervention themselves and not agreeing that the legal mandate is soundly based (for example, the case of a parent who continues to deny that they have abused their child when a court has decided that they did). Task-centred work is not immediately applicable in such circumstances, although with skill there may be ways to move to task-centred practice by obtaining genuine agreement to the legitimacy of intervention (Rooney, 1988b).These are very difficult situations to handle and more work on establishing what proportion of the work they occupy and how they can be kept to a minimum would be very valuable.

Summary

The judgement of the worth of task-centred practice will depend on the value put on open and accountable practice, research-minded work, and the need for a technology which spans care and control and is attractive to clients. The judgement should also be based on the model's compatibility with other systematic approaches. For example, community care planning, welfare rights advocacy, counselling around issues of loss and change, behavioural programmes, locally based practice and community social work all have substantial contributions to make if evaluated under each of the headings of ethics, research and practicality. Task-centred work is compatible with all these approaches. It can also form a framework within which they can take place. The soundness of its claim to stand alongside, or to frame, other approaches should be evident by the end of this book.

2 The Mandate for Work

Introduction

Social work stands at the crossroads between help and control. It is a publicly-sanctioned job which, by necessity, gives a lot of freedom to individuals to interpret these sanctions in practice. Interpretation is a subtle exercise, with shades of meaning seldom made explicit, so it is not surprising that it is often difficult to know how *social sanction* should be translated into action. What is it that sanctions a social worker when he or she makes contact with a client? What processes lead to a person becoming 'a client'? How are these processes influenced by the way in which the social worker interprets the mandate for work?

Who is the client?

When a patient consults with a doctor, or a defendant with a solicitor, it seems clear who the customer is. The same is true of the person who appoints an accountant or hires a painter-decorator. We think in terms of encounters between individuals and see the client in these circumstances as the person who is making particular requests. If there seems to be no ambiguity about who is making the request in these circumstances, why do we need to ask *who is the client* in social work encounters?

This question has been unavoidable since clients gained the right to have access to their case records. The agency discovers that it is not straightforward who should have access to the case file and, therefore, that it is not obvious who the client is. Can it be possible that, for all these years, agencies have been collecting statistics and case returns with names of people who are not 'clients'? (see Doel and Lawson, 1986 and Øvretveit, 1986).

Each time a new file is created there is an implicit answer to the question *who is the client?* in the name or names written on the spine. At first it seems obvious that the file should be available to the person it is named after; if it has Mrs Smith's name on the spine, she is the client and she should have access to it. However, the name of the record is often a simplifying device rather than a carefully made choice, a fact exposed by the close scrutiny needed to make a decision about who should have access to the record. *Who really is the client?* We know that most social work files contain information about people not named on the cover and that some files are named after individuals who are unable to understand its contents. Can a tiny baby truly be considered to be a client?

It is important to stress that the question *who is the client?* is exposed, rather than created by the issue of access to records. Open records highlight dilemmas which were less visible and easier to fudge, but which were nevertheless always present. In this respect, client access has helped us to clarify our thinking and our practice about the mandate for social work intervention.

In Chapter 1 we argued that social work is made up of a number of different jobs spanning care and control. Its main focus and its main tool is problem-solving. As we shall see in Chapter 3 the first stage of problem-solving is problem exploration, during which the worker usually finds that problems involve a number of people.

Individuals can become identified as 'a problem' and one of the worker's first jobs is to move the problem away from the person and into the behaviour, and then from the behaviour to the inter-relationship of behaviours involving a number of people.This process is similar to re-framing in family therapy (Gorrell-Barnes, 1984). In this respect the client is not elderly Mrs Brown, nor Mrs Brown's confused behaviour, but the impact of Mrs Brown's confused behaviour on her neighbours and family. In addition, it is the impact of the behaviour of neighbours and family on Mrs Brown. We can soon see why the case file named 'Mrs Brown' seems an inadequate description for 'the client'.

Case files highlight one aspect of the question *who is the client?* and developments in theory and practice have highlighted others.

For example, developments in family therapy and radical psychiatry in the 1960s broadened our view of who is the client. The medical orthodoxy which focused on individual pathology was challenged by Laing and Esterson (1964), who worked with the whole family as the client; this expressed his view that mental ill-health was a social phenomenon rather than an individual disease. With this interpretation, the client was not the individual but the family.

In the 1970s, the application of systems theory to social work practice (for example, Pincus and Minahan, 1973) helped practitioners to think in a strategic and systematic way about the focus of efforts for change and on whose behalf these efforts are made. Using systems theory, the unitary model of practice challenged the belief in the simple boundaries for the worker's relationship with the client, whether as individual or as family. Instead, the notion of a *client system* broadened the worker's field of action; more importantly, it divorced the word 'client' from a particular person or persons and linked it to the idea of *purpose*. It stressed the skills needed to agree a clear sense of common purpose through negotiation. With this interpretation, the client is defined by the nature of the purpose rather than by the nature of the persons agreeing the purpose.

Whose purpose?

Social work is blessed or blighted, depending on your view, with a further complexity which forces us to ask *who is the client*? There are a number of people who get defined as clients who do not wish to be clients (Rooney, 1988b, calls them involuntary clients), and these numbers seem to be increasing. In the fields of child protection, mental health and dementia, social workers are engaged with people who cannot be called clients by any dictionary definition of the word (according to the *Concise Oxford English Dictionary*, a client is *a person using services of professional man* [sic] – *lawyer, architect, social worker, etc., customer*). The purposes of the work required by the people whose names appear on the spines of case records may be very unclear, or totally at odds with the purposes as seen by the practitioner. In these circumstances, how can they be called clients?

We should not underestimate the impact of this dilemma on the nature of the job. House painting would have a very different image if painter-decorators had statutory powers to practise their trade!

They, too, might feel queasy about *who is the customer*? if they had obligations to respond to callers who made forcible complaints about the state of their neighbour's external paintwork. Although elements of compulsion are shared by some other jobs, most notably the police, social work is perhaps unique in continuing to call the people who do not ask for its services, 'clients'. If the police used this term in similar circumstances it would be laden with irony.

We have seen earlier that the systems approach helps to unlock the question, *who is the client*? by linking it with the notion of purpose. If the purposes are clear, either because of the lucidity of the persons requesting help or because of the explicitness of a legal order, the identity of the client is unambiguous. The difficulties do not arise with clients who may be considered to lie at each end of a continuum; *the applicants* making purposeful and voluntary contact with the agency, or *the mandated clients* subject to explicit legal sanctions (Reid, 1978). What is problematic, in terms of defining the client and interpreting the mandate for work is the large, ill-defined middle of this continuum, where the worker is unsure whether there is a basis for voluntary involvement, but feels cause for concern.

There are four ways in which purpose may be 'knotted' in such a way as to defeat initial efforts to define the client.

- *Clarity of the request for help*
  A person may know that they want help but be unclear what they want help with. There may be so many problems that the person feels defeated by them, or at a loss to know where to begin, and the initial request for help may be reshaped by discussion with the practitioner. Feelings of vague unease or depression may not easily crystallize into a specific request for help.

- *Acknowledgement of the problems*
  A person may not understand or be aware of problems which others have signalled. Factors which the practitioner considers have a significant bearing on the person's situation may not be acknowledged or may be actively denied.

- *Problems involving other people*
  A person may approach the agency with a problem associated with somebody else's behaviour, such as an abusive neighbour. The person only feels that they have a problem in so far as

another person is causing it, so that the scope of the problem lies outside the person's direct control.

- *Ability of the agency to respond.*
  A person may be clear about the help needed but the agency may not be able to respond, either because it does not have the resources or because its purpose as expressed through its policies does not include the kind of help which is requested.

Reid (1978. pp. 309–14) has suggested a classification of problems which helps to demarcate these four issues, all of which must be addressed in order to help the practitioner decide who the client is.

Work with 'the willing' and 'the unwilling'

'Helping' models of practice are under threat for a number of reasons. The first is related to the insensitive application of therapeutic models of practice to clients who do not want the therapy, with ridiculous and sometimes dangerous consequences. The game of enforced therapy was exposed by Mayer and Timms (1970) who described the charades played by clients to satisfy their social worker's desire to *casework* in order to receive the material help they really wanted. The social worker's purpose was to practise casework, the client's was to get some money and the clients became unwilling recipients of the therapeutic service.

Thorpe et al. (1980) described the effects of the broadening of the welfare net in the 1970s which trapped thousands of young offenders who would have been better left untouched by the helpers. The colonization of juvenile justice by social welfare activists had disastrous consequences for the liberty of many young people.

These studies have rightly taught the social work profession to beware using therapeutic models of practice with unwilling customers. It has led to increases rather than decreases in the oppression already experienced by these groups of clients. However, the price paid in the successful battle with the militant therapists has been an almost complete split between work with two different 'kinds' of person – the people who want contact with a social worker and the people who do not.

A further threat to the helping models in social work is the view that an increasingly significant part of the job involves decisions about care, protection and custody. Since it is supposed that work with *the unwilling* is both on the increase and of higher priority, there is every danger that the helping models of practice associated with *the willing* are becoming marginalized.

The division between *the willing* and *the unwilling* results in a similar divide in the kind of work which practitioners feel can be done. This is not necessarily an explicit decision, but we would suggest that it has led to a view that helping models of practice, whether based on psychodynamic or learning theories, are appropriate for *the willing* and that other forms of practice, often not specified in detail, are required for *the unwilling*. Although this has had its most noted success in the field of juvenile justice, where the management of delinquency through diversion stemmed the rise in youth custody, there are few examples of such success.

The task-centred model of practice must encompass work with *the willing* and work with *the unwilling* if it claims to be useful to practitioners. We hope to show that it does.

The model

Taking soundings

The distinction between *the willing* and *the unwilling* is not as clear as we have been suggesting. A model of practice needs to take into account the fact that people's responses will vary, with some becoming more willing to engage in the work and others less so. Task-centred practice builds in the idea of review, a kind of *loop* which at various stages in the model enables workers and clients to backtrack and revise.

After the first contact, which will often have come from somebody who is not named as the client, the worker needs to take soundings to see if further work is appropriate. As we have seen, in cases where there is no clear mandate the worker may need to take many soundings, going back over the work before it is clear whether it should continue. These three factors guide the practitioner in deciding whether further work can or should take place:

- *Clarity of client's purpose*
  If the factors described above (clarity of the request for help; acknowledgement of the problems; problems involving other people; ability of the agency to respond) are positive or are

showing signs of becoming positive, work can take place on an agreed basis, in partnership.

- *Legal mandate*
  If the agency has statutory authority and responsibilities in relation to named clients, work must take place within that legal framework. However, task-centred practice provides a model of social work which is common to work with voluntary and involuntary clients. This bridges the divide between work with *the willing* and *the unwilling*.

- *Clarity of worker's purpose*
  There are circumstances where there is cause for concern about a person's health or safety, but no acknowledgement by these persons or their carers of the grounds for the concern and no basis for legal action. The worker may need to take extensive soundings, regularly reviewing the work, before it becomes clear whether there is a mandate for intervention. This is perhaps the most difficult area for social workers, so we have included a case example in this and subsequent chapters in order to illustrate the model used in this kind of practice.

There is a sense in which it is never possible to work with people who are completely unwilling. If the authority of a court order has to be imposed by force, none of the methods which we call 'social work' are appropriate. Some degree of willingness, some *modus operandi*, is necessary before any social work is possible. The client may not agree with the worker's involvement but they *accept* it.

A dry run

Central to task-centred practice is the belief that the client's own understanding of the model increases its effectiveness, so that practitioners need to be able to describe the process of the work as well as the anticipated outcome. It is not, therefore, a tool to be used *on* a client, but one to be used *with*, and eventually *by*, the client.

For this reason, it is helpful for the client to have an example of the way in which the practitioner intends to work. Before embarking on the detailed examination of problems and the formal written agreement described in the next chapters, the worker and the client may decide to do some work together which gives a foretaste of the working style which the client can expect. This has precedents in many kinds of groupwork, where group members may agree to come to the first one or two sessions with no commitment to further attendance. After that group members may be expected to make a formal decision about continued membership (Heap, 1985).

This *dry run* is particularly helpful when there is conflict between people, often between the generations. A single parent and her adolescent son are at loggerheads with each other and their purposes in any work with the practitioner are far from clear. However, at the end of the initial interview, they agree that they will make two lists – one describing what they find most annoying or hurtful about the other, and the second describing what they find most satisfying or helpful (even if this is from the past!). This gives them a chance to sample the kind of work which is on offer, and it also helps the worker to make an interim decision about who the clients (in terms of people rather than purposes) might be.

At some point the question *who is the client*? has to be answered, or at least closed, even if the point of closure does appear to be arbitrary. The notion of purpose should help the worker to decide which persons are likely to be included in the *client system*; however, it is better to make an imperfect decision than none at all, or allow one to be made by default. The experience of the *dry run* will enable the people involved to review the decision about who the clients are and what mandate there is for further work.

Values

In the final analysis, the mandate for work rests on values. For example, the client's purposes may be very clear, but they may affront the worker's professional code in such a way that no mandate is possible. When the worker's own purposes are used to sanction the work, it is the values on which the intervention is founded which succeed or fail in confirming that mandate. These values must be made explicit so that they can be open to public challenge.

We will see in the following case example how the mandate for work arises within the values which legitimate social work action. We shall also see the benefits which derive from being open and explicit about these values.

The mandate for work – case example

A local Councillor has written to the Social Services in response to a letter she received from the son of Mrs Wall, one of the Councillor's constituents. The letter complains about the behaviour of Mrs Wall's immediate neighbour, Mrs Northwich.

Mrs Northwich is eighty years old and lives on her own in a small terraced house. She finds it difficult to manage stairs, so her bed is in the front room and she has a commode in the same room. Her husband died many years ago and her son lives in a distant city. Mrs Northwich's behaviour is very confused. She often speaks as though her husband is still alive, she forgets to feed herself and she occasionally wanders around the neighbourhood, though she finds her way home.

Mrs Northwich has a home help and home warden who visit her twice daily, helping to maintain her in her own home. They shop, cook, wash and clean for her. During the weekdays, the warden takes her to a local Day Centre for older people who are mentally infirm.

Mrs Wall is also eighty years old. She is mentally alert, but suffers from nervous depression and has become extremely upset by Mrs Northwich, whom she claims knocks on her door at all times of the evening and night and sometimes shouts obscenities at her. No other neighbour claims to be troubled in this way by Mrs Northwich, who used to clean for Mrs Wall many years ago. Mrs Wall also complains that Mrs Northwich's cats dirty her yard. She is adamant that she wants Mrs. Northwich taken away, and this demand is reinforced aggressively by her son who lives on the other side of the city and gets frequent panic telephone calls from his mother.

The referral form names Mrs Northwich as the client.

Who is the client?

Does the social worker have any right or duty to intervene in this situation? If so, what form should it take?

Models of practice which focus on work with the individual may be of limited help in these circumstances, and even if they can be used at some stage, the worker needs a framework which helps to make sense of the broad canvass before any particular individual work can take place.

Let us look at the four areas which we described earlier as key ones to 'unknot' in order to be clear about purpose:

- *Clarity of the request for help*
  The Councillor's request, the son's request and Mrs Wall's request are all too clear. The Councillor wants the Social Services to take action to prevent Mrs Wall from being harassed. Mrs Wall and her son want Mrs Northwich removed from her home and taken into care. At present, we do not know what Mrs Northwich wants and suspect that it might not be easy to find out.

- *Acknowledgement of the problems*
  It is likely that Mrs Northwich may not acknowledge or remember that she is disturbing her neighbour. We do not know whether this is because she suffers from dementia or whether Mrs Wall's account of Mrs Northwich's behaviour is inaccurate. Mrs Wall may not acknowledge that her reaction to Mrs Northwich might be part of the problem. Her son may not acknowledge that his problem is his mother's constant phone calls.

- *Problems involve other people*
  Mrs Wall 'has' the problem, but it involves her neighbour's behaviour. Mrs Northwich only has a problem in so far as her neighbour's actions threaten her independence at home. Her dementia may inhibit her awareness of this threat.

- *Ability of the agency to respond*
  Agencies may respond in ways which do not clarify the work. For example:

  The problem becomes defined as a problem for the agency, so the agency's purpose is self-protective. How can we get the Councillor off our backs? What will help to shut Mrs Wall up? What will satisfy the son sufficient to stop him writing us nasty letters? In these circumstances the agency becomes a *client to itself* and its response is reactive or defensive.

  The agency may define its mandate in narrow terms of physical resources, interpreting its role as a provider of goods: extra hours at the Day Centre, respite care, etc. The proper use of these resources is an essential part of an overall plan, but there are pitfalls in this restricted definition of the agency's purpose. First, if the resources are absent (and frequently they are) this becomes an excuse to withdraw from the work. Secondly, it produces the *pigeon-hole effect* which is characterized by a rapid definition of the problem on the basis of past experience rather than present analysis. So, Mrs Northwich becomes a 'dementia problem' or a 'neighbour problem'. The pigeon-hole effect can appear efficient because it is quick, but it may be ineffective because it is a standardized response, unrelated to the particular situation.

Values in practice

There are no legal requirements for the agency to intervene in this situation. In the final analysis any intervention is based on values. For example:

• respect for a person's right to an independent life at home;
• concern for a person who is suffering distress caused by another;
• concern for a person who may be at risk living at home.

The task-centred practitioner hopes that a better accommodation can be made which compromises neither the respect for independence nor the concern for suffering.

If social workers are not explicit about the value base for their actions it is difficult for others (and for themselves) to understand the foundations of their actions. It is too easy to act on prejudice rooted in a single value statement. The combination of value statements such as those suggested above gives balance to the worker's intervention and reflects the dilemmas which the worker faces. The values do not necessarily justify the intervention, but they do provide a starting point which is open to change and challenge.

The worker has a mandate to intervene with Mrs Northwich and Mrs Wall. The mandate is based on the value statements which we have described and one of the worker's first responsibilities is to try to share this value base with the persons involved, in ways and words which are meaningful to them.

There are two further considerations for the worker before the first contacts are made. The first concerns the priorities in relation to the social worker's other responsibilities – these determine *when* the worker exercises the mandate for work with this case (today, next week, at some time later in the month). The second concerns the technical skills in acting on the mandate – how are the first contacts going to be made, where and with whom?

First steps

There are some technical problems which the worker faces in this case. First and foremost is the ability of Mrs Northwich to reason; if this is severely restricted it limits her ability to understand the process of the work and her ability to defend her own position, which puts her rights at risk. The worker may place equal weight on the values which we have described, but the persons concerned have different power bases. Mrs Wall already has a son and a Councillor to add to the advantage of a lucid mind. Too often, the awareness of this imbalance has led the social worker to 'side with the underdog' and to appear to the Mrs Walls of the world as unsympathetic. The worker needs to be able to protect the power-less whilst giving equal weight to the values behind the work.

In this instance the worker decided to go to the Day Centre to see Mrs Northwich, first on her own and then with her key worker, Janice. The worker found Mrs Northwich's thoughts confused, especially about her husband, whom she believed was still alive, and she was indistinct when the worker mentioned Mrs Wall's complaints. However, Mrs Northwich was very clear that, although she liked to come to the Day Centre, she wanted to continue to live at home – even though her reason was because her husband would not be able to look after himself without her there! Janice supported Mrs Northwich's desire to stay at home and did not feel that she was 'bad enough' to be admitted to the residential home to which the Day Centre was attached. She was aware of a truculent side to Mrs Northwich's nature, but experienced no problems with her behaviour at the Centre.

The worker also saw Mrs Northwich at home with her warden, Sylvia. They had a very easy relationship, but Sylvia was finding it difficult some mornings when Mrs Northwich had 'dirtied herself' and got angry when Sylvia tried to clean her up. Sylvia lived locally and she had seen Mrs Northwich knocking and shouting at Mrs Wall's door. She put this down to the dementia.

After a telephone conversation with Mrs Wall's son, the worker decided to visit Mrs Wall on her own at home. It was clear that the son saw the problem as the frequent and angry telephone calls from his mother, and the worker decided that trying to involve the son more closely in the work could be counter-productive.

Mrs Wall proved able to give chapter and verse about Mrs Northwich's night-time sorties. Usually these consisted of heavy bangings on Mrs Wall's front door, and sometimes they were concluded with abuse through the letter-box ('Why don't you stuff your cat up your . . . ?') The worker felt that Mrs Wall was being truthful, but was equally convinced that her response was contributing to the difficulties; Mrs Wall sat waiting for Mrs Northwich's calls in the evening. She was not concerned about Mrs Northwich's wishes to remain at home.

Conclusion

The case presented by the councillor's letter to the Social Services Department provided no clearcut mandate for the worker's intervention. However, the value statements (page 20) provided a basis from which the worker could take some initial soundings. During these preliminary contacts the worker shared these values, if only in a very limited way, with the persons involved. The worker engaged in a *pre-problem exploration* to get as clear a picture as possible of the facts, as seen by the different parties.

The mandate for work remains uncertain, but the worker has begun to unknot the purposes of the various persons involved in the case and is beginning to form an opinion. The worker hypothesizes that the 'client' is *Mrs Northwich's behaviour in the evenings and Mrs Wall's response to it,* and that the persons likely to be involved are Mrs Wall, Mrs Northwich, Janice (the key worker at the Day Centre) and Sylvia (the warden).

Once the worker has an idea of the scope of the work, it is possible to begin to get a more detailed picture of the nature of the problems. We will examine this phase in the next chapter.

3 Exploring Problems

Introduction

Task-centred practice is based on a clear concept of *problem*. The starting point of the model is the problem; it is not, for example, a child care model nor a groupwork model; it is a *problem-solving* model which has been developed in work with all clients, whether as individuals, families, or groups.

Problems, in task-centred practice, can be considered as the social difficulties that individuals, groups or communities face. These difficulties can derive from the way that people themselves experience their lives and come to regard social issues that face them as problematic ('I'm finding this a problem'). They can also arise because of social behaviour, for example parenting, which falls short of standards which are acceptable ('someone has told me this is a problem'). The concept of problem, at the base of the model, is derived from these two views. For there to be a *problem* either the individual agrees that this is so, or there are formally approved processes (usually courts) that define a situation as problematic for the individual irrespective of that person's wishes. In principle and as a starting point the worker needs to consider whether one or both of these versions of problem is present. If so then there is work to be done. If neither is present then there is unlikely to be work to be done. Social work practice is not of course that simple, as we have seen in the previous chapter and as we will see in the case example at the end of this one, but the clear allocation of *problem* to one or other category should be taken as a yardstick against which to measure the clarity of work.

If there is a problem the work to resolve it will be undertaken by client and worker in the task phase of the model. In order to generate these tasks, and in order for them to have a reasonable chance of resolving the client's difficulties, the problem itself must be relatively specific. It needs to have limits to it which allow it to be demarcated from other problems that the client faces (which might need different activities to resolve) and so it needs to be phrased in such a way that it is clear to both worker and client what it includes and what it excludes.

The problem must also be one which is capable of resolution by the client and worker. For example, there is little point in a mother agreeing with the social worker that the problem is the behaviour of her teenage son if he is totally unwilling to change that behaviour. There is also little point in a worker and client agreeing to deal with debt problems if there has already been a substantial debt counselling programme undertaken elsewhere, and little realistic hope of improvement beyond the work already done. It is vitally important in task-centred work that agreed problems are ones that can potentially be dealt with and that the parties to the agreement have a legitimate claim to deal with them.

The process of problem exploration

An accurate definition of problem involves a number of elements in problem exploration, beginning with an introduction into the work, moving on to scanning all potential problems, and then giving some detail to them and selecting ones to work on. This is the sequence which will be described stage by stage below. It is a logical sequence but in practice the neat movement from one stage to the next is deflected by many factors. Clients may need to cover things a number of times in order to get through emotionally fraught issues. Workers may realize that they have not completed earlier stages as well as they should have and want to backtrack. Many other matters may intervene and complicate the neat order of events. With the best task-centred practice this will not be evident to the client. The client should experience a constructive process of getting problems into clearer focus – they will not notice the way that a number of other matters, such as their tears over a past loss or their angry feelings over some recent event, have been sympathetically handled in the midst of this problem exploration sequence.

The model

Problem exploration consists of an initial broad sketch followed by more detailed examination. The various problems need separating and then putting into some order so that the most important is evident and the whole picture makes sense for the client and the worker. A useful metaphor for this is the production of the *front page* of a newspaper. There are headlines and detailed stories, and the page layout needs deciding in the light of which story is to be the lead. Direct quotes to illustrate and sum up the story line are also important. All these items and processes play their part in task-centred problem exploration.

In this metaphor the initial work is the scanning for headlines. This is followed by the consideration of any additional headlines that may be needed and then by the storylines that will accompany each headline. Quotes from the client will be useful and finally the page layout work will involve the selection of lead stories and the allocation of appropriate prominence to headlines, stories and quotes in the light of this selection. It is possible to envisage in your mind the *front page* taking shape as the process of problem exploration unfolds.

Introducing the model

In task-centred practice the client should be clear at all stages what is happening to them and why. The exact purpose of any question may not be evident to the client, but the general purpose of the discussions that they are having should be known to them. No question should come as a bolt out of the blue, although of course a number of questions will inevitably be hazily connected to the current stage, for example if the worker is making inspired guesses.

Explaining what you are doing and why is part of the model's emphasis on helping people to help themselves, as well as part of the value system underlying the model. This stresses open practice and the rights of individuals and groups to know what is happening to them when they are receiving a service. It may also aid effective problem-solving (Goldstein, 1973).

There is a natural tendency to provide *all* the information about the model itself at the start of the work. It seems logical and it is a good introduction. It also seems easier for the practitioner: there is a great deal to get through in any task-centred interview and dealing with all the information about the model itself at the start may seem a good way of reducing the many calls on practitioner attention. Unfortunately describing the work in one go is not the best way to handle this from the client's point of view. Going into considerable detail at an early point raises a number of difficulties.

Early on in interviews there is a strong likelihood that a number of issues are dominant in the client's mind – they have come to discuss several things and they want to remember them and cover them. Some or all of these things may be very worrying issues. This is not the best frame of mind for listening to explanations regarding the way that the worker wishes to handle the interview. The internal response to a lengthy introduction is likely to be, 'come on, get on with it, I just want to talk about the things that have brought me here'.

Bear in mind also that this is an early stage of the work. Most workers will be an unknown quantity to their new clients and this will increase general nervousness. Equally, the agency may be new to the client and a source of worry – how does it work, is there any stigma associated with going to it? In addition, it is very likely that the client has arrived at social services after contact with a number of different agencies (Stevenson and Parsloe, 1978; Fisher et al., 1986). Approaches by other professionals are likely to have featured in their lives in connection with the problems you are about to explore. Other explanations of ways of working will have been given and this could be just one more in a wearisome saga.

All in all, it is unlikely to be the ideal time to try and explain how you intend to work. Probably the best solution is a brief introduction, something like, 'I'd like to spend some time with you getting as clear as possible the different problems that we may be able to help with – quite soon we'll see which of them are the most important ones'.

It is usually best if explanations are given in small sections as the work proceeds. Earlier explanations can be repeated to present a cumulative picture of the model: 'Do you remember that I said that we'd try to get all of the possible problems that you might want to work on out on the table right at the start? Now that we've done that, let's go on to look at one or two in a bit more detail.'

Delaying the description of the work may be appropriate at times, for example: 'I know that it's been difficult for you to come in here and we've talked about some things for the last half hour which are obviously very sad for you. Now that you say that you feel a bit better about discussing these things could I just explain a little how I work, as it's very important to me that you know how we're going to go on from here?' Short explanations, carefully timed and with perhaps a brief recap now and again, are likely to be the best introduction to the model.

Scanning for headlines

To return to our metaphor of the production of a newspaper page, the first stage is to scan for all the major headlines that might be used; the process of problem exploration begins with a scan of all the problems that might possibly be tackled in the work between social worker and client. The intention is to get as many of the problems as possible out in the open, and in brief form, so that the range of difficulties can be seen. This stage is not easy to handle. Clients often think that there is one issue so dominant that mentioning anything else is a total waste of time, and workers may be reluctant to raise a problem that they are mandated to cover because they know it is likely to cause an angry reaction. There may also be a long list of problems and this can appear very daunting and dispiriting.

If there is a major issue which the client wishes strongly to cover in detail now then this needs to be respected. It should be regarded as a temporary deflection from the sequence of problem exploration, just as a very upset client might lead you to spend some time being sympathetic or offering brief counselling. Structures are there to help not hinder. Clients will not concentrate on other issues if one dominant concern occupies their thoughts or feelings. The best rule may be to allow interruptions, but always to remember where you left off (Reid and Epstein, 1972).

There are a number of ways that interruptions can occur within a careful scan of the problems. For example, clients may arrive with one immediate concern. Others may mention something which you know to be so pressing that you need to deal with it there and then, for example, a threatened fuel disconnection, or legal proceedings about to occur, which may warrant very quick attention because of the consequences of delay.

Once the scan is complete a number of headlines will be identified by the end. It is very important that the headlines are brief (the case at the end of this chapter includes 'Wandering at night' and 'Getting lost coming back from the day centre'). This period of the work should be a scan and no more – covering the width of the client's concerns, not the depth. There is, of course, no commitment to work on any of these problems until an agreement is made. At present the work consists of a *review* of all of the potential problems as agreed by the client or mandated by others.

Additions

The task-centred worker will have already raised any problems which arise from external mandates (for example, as a result of a court order) and the process of scanning will have covered the problems which the client recognizes and wants to bring to the attention of the worker. However, there may be situations that the worker can see as problems in the client's life but which have not featured in the list. These could derive from the worker's view of the client's life (for example, the teenager who is so upset about a particular issue in a family argument that he does not notice that the relationship with his father also sounds pretty bad). Additional problems may need mentioning because of another agency's concerns which the client is ignoring, or is possibly ignorant of (for example, the Education Welfare Service may have visited the teenager because of poor school attendance – but this is not yet at the stage of a mandated problem). In terms of our newspaper metaphor these problems may become additional headlines for the page.

These additions to the list of problem headlines need to be raised, but they cannot be compulsory additions to the agreed work. They are for negotiation and discussion. At the end of the day the only problems on the *front page* which will result in action are those which the client agrees should be acted upon, and those where an external mandate enforces and legitimates action.

Problem details – the storylines

At this stage we should have a list of brief problem headlines.

An elderly person may be: *unable to manage shopping.*

A teenage son may agree that there are: *constant arguments between me and my mum about late nights.*
An adult on a supervision order may worry that: *too much drinking will lead to trouble with the law again.*
A couple may have: *fuel bills and private debts that cannot be met.*

These are problem headlines, they are not detailed and they do not imply solutions. It is all too easy to think in terms of solutions at this stage. Many clients arrive with solutions in mind, and it can be very tempting to make a quick connection between a stated problem and an apparently obvious solution ('You can't manage your shopping, I'll fix up a home help'). This is to be avoided. There is not enough information to be confident about solutions proposed by either you or the client, nor is there enough information for the impact of a solution to be clear to worker or client. What is needed now are the details of the problem, the storyline behind the headlines so that the worker, and the client, can assess the severity and scale of the difficulty, and decide who needs to be involved in any attempted resolution.

First, is it one problem, or is it really two or more? Each problem needs to be clear enough for the worker and the client to see if it should be divided into different problems. 'The constant arguments between me and my mum mean that I stay out late at night' – are there problems about the relationship between mum and teenager *accompanied* by problems about what happens 'when I stay out at night'? If work is carried out on one problem when really there are two the work is likely to be less effective.

Secondly, what is the scale of this problem? How constant are the 'constant' arguments? The worker and the client need to get a reasonable idea of the severity of the problem, in order for an assessment to be made by both of them of the importance of the different problems that are being raised. Towards the end of this exploratory stage problems will be put in priority for action and an idea of the scale of the different problems is important. Sometimes this process will uncover the fact that a problem is not as bad as the client initially thought – 'Well, I suppose that we've only had one argument this week, but it seems like it's all the time'. This may still be a very bad problem, but the judgement of the severity of it needs to be informed by some basic idea of its scale as well as its perceived impact on the client's life.

Lastly, who needs to agree that this is a problem? If the teenager can do something on his or her own about the arguments then the teenager can agree and define the problem. If the mother needs to change (in the teenager's eyes), then she needs to be involved in the discussion and involved in the problem definition.

The problem headlines should have enough detail added to them for it to be clear that each one is a problem in its own right. The scale of the problem should be clear. The definition of the problem should be within the capacity of the people with whom the worker is negotiating. In short, a storyline should have been established, and it is now missing just one vital element – a quote from the client.

Problem statements – a client quote

The model is attempting to reduce any gap between the worker's understanding of the problem and the client's, and a direct quote from the client helps this process. The client's own words are important in order to establish the shared understanding and to base the model firmly in the client's own world. Providing a direct quote reinforces the commitment inherent in this model to tackle ethnocentric (and discriminatory) assumptions (see, for example, Nofz (1988) who provides a useful example of the ways in which the task-centred approach may be based on the values of different cultures within a society).

We had a headline earlier for the case with a teenager who agreed that there were *constant arguments between me and my mum about late nights*. A quote may be added after careful discussion such as the following:

Teenage son, with mother's agreement: 'My mum and I don't like the arguments when I stay out late with friends.'

The problem statement consists of these three parts: a headline, a storyline and a quote.

Selection

The clients now need to put this list of problems in priority order. If a mandated problem exists, it must be the first priority. For example, in the course of preparation of a Social Enquiry Report for a court it may have been agreed that the major reason that a juvenile was getting into trouble was his evenings spent with a particular group of friends. This may have resulted in a problem statement, following on from the making of a supervision order, something like this, 'The juvenile supervision order means that you must not get into trouble – this has been with particular friends in the evening and alternatives will need to be found'. This, as a mandated problem, would automatically be selected top priority. There is no option in dealing with this and it needs to come number one in the list, but the other priorities are the client's own, derived after discussion with the worker. The worker's role is to help the client to select problems in an informed way, for example, suggesting what might logically come first and pointing out the urgency of some issues. 'At the end of the process it is the client's view of priority which needs to prevail.

Some clients may be reluctant to see any problem as more important than any other ('they're all important to me'). However, with some discussion it is usually possible to achieve a more realistic view. Everyone has some way of deciding what they really want to tackle next and the work at this stage is to unlock that for the client.

The task-centred model is concerned with motivation of the client. The problems which the client has to work on (because they are mandated) or wants to work on (because they have chosen them and given a priority to them) are the ones that are most linked to motivation. The worker may disagree with the order suggested and point this out and discuss the reasons, but the final order of the problems, apart from those with an external mandate, is the client's.

Lead problems

The list of problems is now in priority order and one or more problems needs to be selected to focus on in the work. The research on the model suggests that a limited number of problems should be worked on at any one time (see, for example, Blizinsky and Reid, 1980). Up to three may be a suitable maximum. For each problem there will be associated goals and tasks as we will see in later chapters. Too many selected problems will probably lead to confusion and dissipated effort. The necessity to begin somewhere will already have been established in the discussion of priority – the selection of one or more problems builds on that discussion. In newspaper terms it is the *selection* of the *lead story or stories* for the front page.

Some explanation is likely to be useful at this stage to point out that no problem need be lost forever, it is just a case of tackling things in order (a worker may need to say something like, 'we will return to the other problems later if you want that, but we do need to begin somewhere'). The workers may point out that this way of working is known to be effective, and that tackling too much at once risks not achieving much at all ('it's my experience that working on one or two issues at the start is by far the best way; let's make sure that we're getting somewhere on the top issues and then we can move on'). It may be useful to bear in mind that achieving a small success is likely to be much better than achieving a spectacular failure. For many distressed people achieving a small success is very important indeed.

The inside story

There is now a lead problem, or perhaps lead problems. Some further details may need exploring before action can be taken, perhaps also involving some discussions with other workers or family members. In newspaper terms this will be the *inside story*.

'My mum and I don't like the arguments that occur when I stay out late with friends.' What is the full nature of this problem? When does it usually occur, what precedes it, what follows it, how long has it been a problem? The details of the problem need spelling out. This is made complicated by the fact that the people describing the problem may not know some of the details (for example, few of us keep a daily diary of the rows that we have with our children) and also the fact that assumptions are always made about the listener's knowledge of characters and events in the problem. This stage, where the analysis is changing gear and going into depth rather than width, will always benefit from examples. 'Could you just describe the most recent argument to me?' 'Would you just go back over the past week with me and see when the arguments occurred?' 'Let's just take that example and look what happened just before it.' 'Could you give me an example of what you mean by his friends "getting into trouble"?'

Questions that cover behaviour, and questions that establish detail are to be encouraged at this stage, and professional jargon is to be avoided. The worker might end up with something like this at the end of this phase:

> The arguments involve a lot of shouting. I (the son) think that my mum is unfair about my life and my friends. I (the mother) think that the arguments are going to get violent. We usually know that they are going to happen because I (the son) need to borrow money to go out and this leads to the row. I (the son) don't see why my mum should know where I am if I'm out late, and I don't agree that my friends are getting into trouble and that I will get into trouble if I carry on going out with them.

Supplementing and corroborating

Reid and Epstein (1972) describe the problems which the client has selected as target problems. These may be fully defined by the parties to the discussion, but it may be that some extra information is required to supplement that which has been given, or possibly to corroborate it. Any such information should be gathered with the client's agreement (although this may need to be waived if mandated problems are being investigated). Some information of this sort may be gathered at this stage by breaking off the discussion for a telephone call, or by asking someone else in the family to join in briefly. It is important that it is done as fast as possible so that action on the problem can occur soon. It is also important that it is done as a supplement to, and not a substitute for, the client's views.

Only an external mandate for problems

The situation can arise that, after a problem scan, the only problems are the ones that the social worker has raised as mandated ones. This is not a common situation but it does occur. What situations are these likely to be? There may be times when clients change their minds about agreeing to do work on problems, and the social worker is left with just the externally mandated problem. For example, people may suggest that they want to work on problems because of a number of perceived advantages to them in doing so. The prospective probationer, who seems willing to work on a number of problems before the making of the supervision order, can decide that they are remarkably problem-free once the supervision order is made! People may also feel that they are expected to work on problems because of some family or other social pressure. An elderly woman may agree to a number of problems when her daughter is present but slowly remove them from the list after her daughter has left. Finally, there may be no real discussion beyond the mandated problem because of basic disagreement about the externally mandated problem itself. An investigation of child abuse leading to client anger and distrust may lead the parents to reject any need for help because of their rejection of the externally mandated problem. The probationer, and the parents suspected of child abuse, will have to tolerate further involvement by the worker, the elderly woman (assuming no agreed problems and no external mandate) will not.

In the case of probation (and any supervision order where the client does not want to work on any voluntary problem) the worker is left with an attempt to enforce action on unwilling clients. Agreeing on the fact that the order is a nuisance (or worse!) to the client and therefore on the need to remove the mandated problem may be a way forward (Rooney, 1988b). If this can be done then there is scope for task-centred work. If this can't be done then the worker is faced with a client who is unwilling to act on the mandated problem and who, in other circumstances, would not continue as a client. It is possible to continue with the spirit of task-centred work in this case but it cannot be called task-centred practice. Continuing in the spirit of the model would involve maintaining the attempts at participation, openness and honesty and repeatedly attempting to re-engage the client in properly agreed work on the mandated problem (Fisher, 1990). It is likely, though, that the worker will be monitoring actions in the client's world and instructing rather than negotiating about changes of behaviour.

There are limits to helping those who are 'sentenced to help' (Bottoms and MacWilliams, 1979). Task-centred probation officers, and others who supervise orders for criminal offences, regularly find these limits. The task-centred model helps to establish limits that respect the effectiveness (or rather lack of it) of compulsory help (Marshall, 1987) and the need to respect an individual's right to refuse that help if they wish. Social control functions will be the only ones to be carried out in such cases. These functions may also be present in child protection cases where a mandated problem exists regarding the welfare of the child but, as in the Probation example, if there is no agreement on problems and no acceptance of mandated problems, it cannot be said to be task-centred practice.

From individual to family and group

Problem exploration will often involve families or groups – how does this affect the tasks involved? The short answer is that all the basic principles still apply (Garvin, 1974). There needs to be some introduction to the model's stages, a scan of problems, more detailed definition, ranking and selection of problems. It may be possible to conduct all of this with the group or family as if they were an individual client and come to a group understanding of problems; alternatively there may be some individual elements within the group approach (for a discussion and examples of many of these issues see Fortune, 1985). Let us consider the two possible outcomes of, first, group agreement and then, group agreement *and* individual agreement.

Outcome one, a group (or family) agreement: the situation where the group comes to a common answer to all the different elements of problem exploration. The stages would proceed, after some brief introduction, with the group discussing the range of problems that they were facing, defining them as a group, giving them priority as a group, and selecting problems as a group. A task-centred worker would be making sure that all relevant problems were covered (being particularly aware in these circumstances of group pressure to hide or to reveal certain problems), and problems would be checked to make sure that dealing with them was within the ability of the group (Larsen and Mitchell, 1980), exactly as in individual work. There may be dissent within the group at any of these stages; for example, one group member might not want a particular problem included in the problem scan because they did not regard this as a problem for themselves – this could lead to a different outcome.

What happens if part way through the problem scan with a family the teenage son says that, in spite of his parents' view, he does not agree that his choice of friends is a problem? What do you do? There are a number of possible ways forward in this situation. Deciding which is best will depend on the circumstances facing you; there is no clear order to the options. The first is to see if the family group can still come to a joint agreement on the issue. A judgement needs to be made as to the likelihood of change on the part of the dissenting individual. This judgement may lead to a redefinition of the problem in such a way that everyone can agree to the new version. For example, it may be possible to get agreement to the phrase 'the choice of *some* friends is a problem', rather than 'the choice of *all* friends is a problem'. Clearly this must not be done in such a way that the original problem becomes lost in the process of redefinition; it could become so watered down that the real problem is no longer covered by the new one. However, if it can be done, then a family group agreement is still possible; if it cannot be done, separate agreements with group members will be needed.

Outcome two, individual *and* group agreement: the parents may agree that they want to work on this problem but the son will not. The basic principle of task-centred work, that the resolution of the problem must be possible, will still apply. The parents are unlikely to be in a position, either practically or ethically, to control their teenage son's choice of friends. They might agree a problem which was something like this, 'we do not approve of some of our son's friends, we want to consider exactly why this is and what we would like to do as good parents'. One value of group discussion of this kind of problem may be that parents can see more clearly the limits imposed on their actions by the unwillingness of others to agree with their views. Reaching a redefined problem, as in the example above, may be very difficult indeed unless the relevant parties can see that their preferred option is completely unrealistic. This option of the redefined problem may apply to a smaller group (as in our example of the parents), or it may apply to an individual (perhaps just one of the parents wants to stick with this as a problem and work on it for themselves).

The balance of group and individual problems is important. It may be the case that there is very limited scope for group definition of problems and a series of separate individual discussions will be held (which the group may aid). There is nothing inherently better about a group understanding of the problem, although there may be circumstances where progress is very unlikely without such an understanding (some family situations may need group agreement for any long-lasting solutions). If it is true that progress will not occur without the group basis then this can be emphasized in the individual work. As progress falters on the individual work so the idea of a group approach may seem more acceptable to the parties concerned, and there will be the chance to reintroduce the group view with evidence from the activities so far that the individual version is not making progress.

A final note on terminology – *the client*

Task-centred theory contains careful definitions of the various components of the model: *problem, scan, explore*, and so on. This is a very important part of any model; the theory can only advance if those using it employ common terms and common definitions. Unfortunately, social work has often been sloppy in its use of language and a careful eye needs to be kept by the task-centred practitioner on the correct use of the terms in the model. Ideally this accuracy should extend to that over-used term *client*, an issue we have already noted in Chapter 2 concerning the question 'who is the client?'. A final word on this issue would be valuable.

People who receive brief advice on duty desks are said to be clients, users of day centres are clients, those receiving compulsory after care in the criminal justice system are clients. Debates are held about the nature of the client in child care cases (when is it the family and when is it the child), and acknowledgement is sometimes made of missing clients, such as carers of elderly people who receive domiciliary services. Task-centred approaches should encourage greater clarity about the term 'client'. We need to be clear on whose behalf we are working, who is defining the problem and on what basis. Some of these issues will not be easily resolved; the rights of different individuals to be heard in a case, who needs to be party to a given agreement and so on. Clarifying who should be involved and how is often a major part of work in any complex case. However, task-centred work in particular has reserved the term *client* for the individual (or family or group) who has come to a formal agreement with a practitioner to engage in work. Up to that point those seeking help have not been considered as clients within the task-centred framework. The term *client* has, therefore, meant someone who is actively engaged in work with the practitioner, and not someone who is discussing that possibility. Moving to client status has marked the change from exploring to doing.

Those who come to seek social work help, and who may become clients, sometimes come in response to others having insisted on their approach (for example a court order) and sometimes they are making an application without this legal pressure. It may be helpful to distinguish these two groups, who are likely to enter into negotiations regarding help with rather different preconceptions, into *respondents* and *applicants*. Someone approaching social services is therefore either a respondent or an applicant, and they may or may not become a client (Reid and Epstein, 1972).

The term *client* is so generally used for people in all phases of engagement with social workers that it may be difficult to convert it to this more precise use. Leaving it as a portmanteau term is not very satisfactory, and it is to be hoped that developments, in community care and child protection, may establish new and more precise usage in years to come.

Exploring problems – case example

This follows work on pages 18–22.

The worker helps the clients discuss their problems at a general level (SCAN for Headlines). This will include any problems identified or suggested by the worker (ADDITIONAL Headlines). Then, together, they look in greater detail at each of these problem areas (DETAIL for Storylines), arriving at a brief STATEMENT (Quote from client) for each problem. Finally, the worker and the clients discuss which problem or problems the clients wish to reduce the most (SELECTION for lead story); there may be MORE DETAIL for the Inside Story on the Selected Problem.

We will use the newspaper *front page* metaphor to describe the work with Mrs Northwich and Mrs Wall.

1 SCANNING for Headlines
Following the work to establish the mandate for work, the worker decides to include Mrs Northwich, Mrs Wall, Sylvia (the warden) and Janice (the day centre worker) in the work.

Scanning problems with Mrs Northwich, helped by Sylvia, the warden:

The following Headlines emerge as problematic:

Increasing incontinence

This is a problem for Sylvia, who has to wash Mrs Northwich each morning, but Mrs Northwich has told Sylvia that she doesn't like 'feeling wet'. The worker sees this problem as an additional threat to Mrs Northwich's independence.

Wandering at night

Mrs Northwich is confused about why she does this and Sylvia says that sometimes Mrs Northwich has said she'd been looking for her husband (who is dead). This is a problem for Mrs Northwich because it makes her scared, and Sylvia and the worker also see the further threat posed to Mrs Northwich's independence.

Mrs Northwich relies on Sylvia and the home help, John, for all her cleaning, shopping and cooking.

Scanning problems with Mrs Northwich, helped by Janice, the day centre worker:

Getting lost going home from the day centre

The day centre for the mentally infirm is a five minute walk for Mrs Northwich and she enjoys going there each day. Janice says that she gets on well with the other people, with only rare incidents of the abuse which Mrs Wall describes. However, staff are worried about her making her own way home (Sylvia often brings her in the mornings), because she has got lost.

The worker has tried to find out directly from Mrs Northwich what, if anything, she finds problematic, but has had to rely on Sylvia and Janice, both of whom seem to have Mrs Northwich's well-being in mind. They have had the opportunity to talk with her at more lucid moments and both have confirmed that Mrs Northwich likes the day centre but wants to stay at home with her cats as long as she can. The worker infers that anything which threatens this is a problem to Mrs Northwich.

Scanning problems for Headlines with Mrs Wall

Upsetting behaviour in the evenings

Mrs Wall spends a lot of time letting off steam about what she has had to put up with and how the situation has been getting worse over the last few months.

Cats messing the yard

Mrs Wall complains about the smell and the dirt from her neighbour's undisciplined cats and feels that it is cruel to keep animals in such conditions.

2. ADDITIONAL Headlines

Picking up on a brief reference to a local church group which Mrs Wall used to attend, the worker initiates a discussion about social activities and wonders if another problem Headline could be

Social life restricted

Mrs Wall's response is ambiguous. The worker asks to jot a brief note down, as a reminder perhaps to return to this area and decides to take Mrs Wall's non-committal answer as a 'yes'.

The worker avoids the considerable temptation to become solutional with Mrs Wall, 'have you thought about . . . ?' in the knowledge that this would draw the response, 'yes, but . . .'. At this point Mrs Wall wants somebody to feel the quality of her misery: she is not about to entertain any solution other than the removal of Mrs Northwich. The worker finds it hard to like Mrs Wall.

3 DETAILS for Storyline

arriving at

4 STATEMENT, Quote from client

The worker looks at each problem Headline in detail, getting a Quote from the client which summarizes each Headline. In this case we illustrate this process with three of the Headlines.

Getting lost going home from the day centre

(Headline identified by Janice)

When did this occur? In fact only twice, as far as Janice can remember, and these were during the last few weeks. She had no exact record of which days.

What happened? Mrs Northwich usually leaves the day centre after tea at about half past five, but on these two occasions she wasn't at home when Sylvia, the warden, went to get her ready for bed at 7.00 pm. Sylvia went to look for her and found her wandering locally on waste ground.

Why did it happen? Mrs Northwich is confused, so perhaps she just got lost. However, after careful questioning, it emerged that staff shortages may have contributed, because on these two occasions

Mrs Northwich had lingered in the television room and had not been reminded to go home until after dark.

Janice says that it would be possible for Mrs Northwich to stay at the day centre into the evening on a planned, regular basis, but it is now early November and the evenings and late afternoons are already getting darker.

The *consequences* of this problem continuing are that Mrs Northwich's use of the day centre will be increasingly restricted as winter approaches and an opportunity to make more use of the day centre will be lost.

This problem becomes redefined and clarified into the following statement, a quote from Janice: '*Mrs Northwich is likely to get lost going home when it is dark.*'

Upsetting behaviour in the evenings

(Headline identified by Mrs Wall)

What behaviours are problematic?
Mrs Wall produces a carefully maintained diary which chronicles incidents over the last three months. The diary indicates that Mrs Northwich bangs on the front door and shouts obscenities through the letter-box. Apart from being told to stuff a cat somewhere she'd prefer not to mention, Mrs Wall won't elaborate on what the obscenities are.

When? and Where?
Usually between nine and midnight, some weeks almost every evening, then sometimes a week goes by without an incident. Always outside Mrs Wall's front door.

Why is the behaviour a problem?
Obviously, the behaviour is annoying, and Mrs Wall says that the irregularity makes matters worse, because she sits in wait for Mrs Northwich even when she doesn't come. 'When she comes it's a relief, because then it's over.'

Who does the behaviour affect?
Mrs Wall is particularly upset because she feels singled out for this treatment (other people on the street aren't affected). Also, she feels that other people don't believe her and no one will do anything (the police will not get involved). The worker lets Mrs Wall know that Sylvia, the warden, is aware that it happens.

The worker and Mrs Wall discuss what she has done about the behaviours so far, which seems restricted to telephoning other people, like the police and her son at all times of the night. The *consequences* of the continuation of the problem is deepening fear and anxiety and losing contact with her son, who sometimes puts the phone down on her.

This detailed analysis revealed that, although Mrs Northwich's behaviour was the cause, the problem was the fear and distress which Mrs Wall felt each evening in anticipation of the event. In addition, she was hurt by the deterioration in her relationship with her son, Philip. The problem was stated by Mrs Wall as:

'I get fearful and upset every evening waiting for Mrs Northwich to bang and shout at my front door.'

'I don't know what to do to make things better with Philip.'

DETAIL for Storyline about ADDITIONAL Headline

Social life restricted

(Headline identified by the worker)

Towards the end of the time spent looking at the problems in detail, the worker returned to this possible problem area. Mrs Wall agreed that she used to get out more and that she had enjoyed going to a local church group, but that she had lost interest in recent years, and especially since the trouble with Mrs Northwich. She expressed no interest in pursuing this area, and no more details were discussed.

5   SELECTION for Lead Story

The worker felt that there would probably be two parts to any Agreement in this case; the first negotiated with Janice acting on behalf of Mrs Northwich and the second with Mrs Wall. Each party, including Sylvia, would be aware of the full Agreement, not just their own part in it.

Each of the problems identified in the Scan were detailed (we have described only three examples of this). The worker was obliged to discuss inappropriate solutions with Mrs Wall, who had begun the interview demanding that Mrs Northwich be removed from home. To the extent that she still wanted this to happen, it was a goal that was not achievable and one which the worker believed to be undesirable, so could not agree to work towards.

The worker and Janice acting on Mrs Northwich's behalf selected the problem already detailed above and the worker also agreed to contact Mrs Northwich's doctor to see if she could advise about the incontinence. Mrs Wall selected two related problems – her fear and anxiety waiting for Mrs Northwich's banging and her difficulties with her son.

Newspaper metaphor

The *Problem Page* (Figure 3.1) illustrates how the problems in the case example could be represented using the metaphor of the front page of a newspaper, described earlier in this chapter. In some instances the worker might choose to take the metaphor into an actual working exercise.

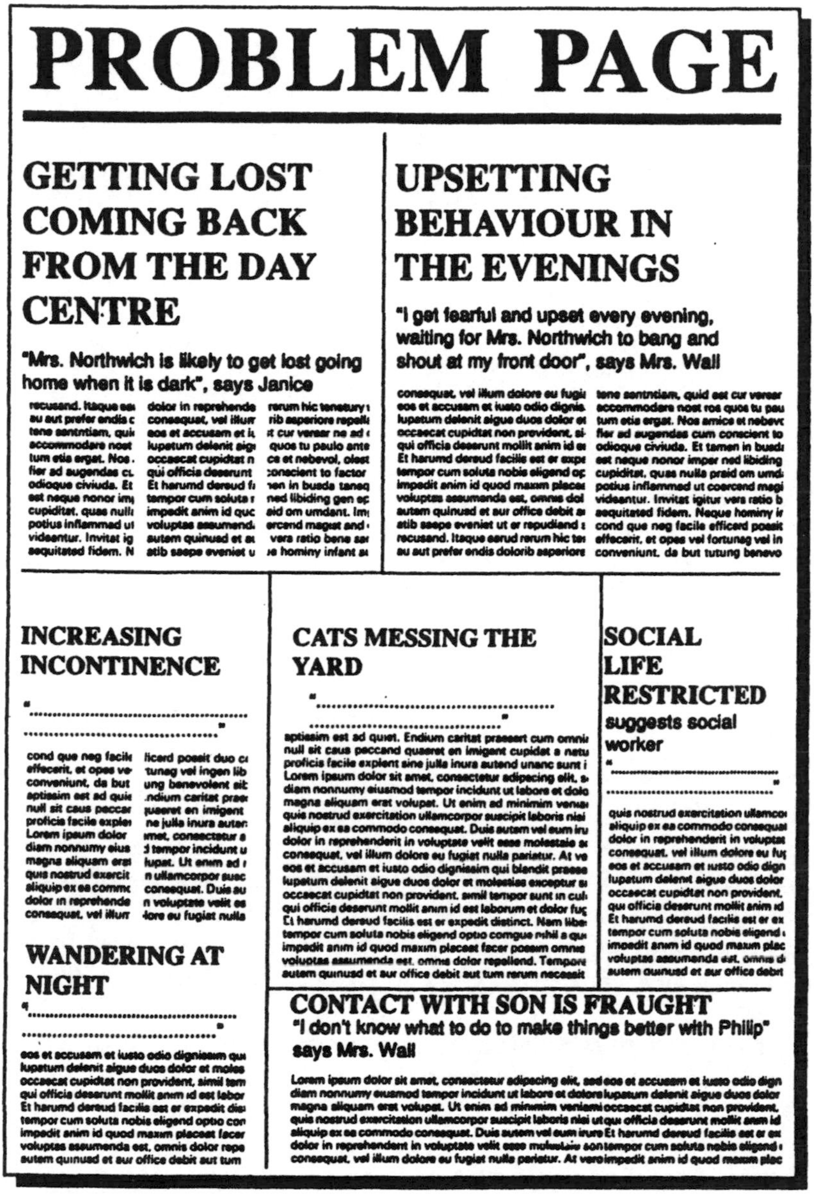

PROBLEM PAGE

GETTING LOST COMING BACK FROM THE DAY CENTRE

"Mrs. Northwich is likely to get lost going home when it is dark", says Janice

recusand. Itaque eet au aut prefer endis c tene sentntiam, qui accommodare nost tum etis erget. Nos . fier ad augendas ct odioque civiuda. Et est neque nonor im cupiditat, quas null potius inflammed ut videantur. Invitat ig sequitated fidem. N

dolor in reprehende consequat, vel illur eos et accusam et i lupetum delenit sig quos tu paulo ante occaecat cupidtat n qui officia deserunt Et harum dereud fi tempor cum solute i impedit anim id quc voluptas assumand autem quinuod et at atib saepe eveniet u

rerum hic tenetury i rib esperiore repell: it cur verear ne ad i ce et nebevol, oiest conscient to factor ten in bueda taneq ned libiding gen oc eid om umdant. Imi ercend maget and i vers ratio bene ser ve hominy infant at

UPSETTING BEHAVIOUR IN THE EVENINGS

"I get fearful and upset every evening, waiting for Mrs. Northwich to bang and shout at my front door", says Mrs. Wall

consequat, vel illum dolore eu fugi: eos et accusam et iusto odio dignis. lupetum delenit aigue duos dolor et occaecat cupidtat non provident, si- qui officia deserunt mollit anim id e: Et harum dereud facilis est er expe tempor cum soluta nobis eligend oc impedit anim id quod maxim placer voluptas assumends est, omne dol autem quinuad et aur office debit a atib saepe eveniat ut er repudiand i recusand. Itaque sarud rerum hic te: au aut prefer endis dolorib asperiore

tene sentntiam, quid est cur verear accommodare nost ros quos tu pau tum etis erget. Nos amice et nebevc fier ad augendas cum conscient to odioque civiuda. Et tamen in bued est neque nonor imper ned libiding cupidtat, quas nulla praid om umdi potius inflammed ut coercend magi videantur. Invitat igitur vers ratio b sequitated fidem. Neque hominy ir cond que neg facile efficard possit effecerit, et opes vel fortunas vel in conveniunt. de but tutung benevo

INCREASING INCONTINENCE

".."

cond que neg facile effecerit, et opes ve convenivnt, de but aptissim est ad quie null sit caus paccar proficia facile exple: Lorem ipsum dolor diam nonnumy eius magna aliquam erat quis nostrud exercit aliquip ex es commc dolor in reprehende consequat, vel illurr

licerd possit duo ci tunag vel ingen lib ung benevolent sit: ndium caritat prae: queeret en imigent ne julla inura auten smet, consectetur a d tempor incidunt u lupat. Ut enim ad i n ullamcorpor susc consequat. Duis au n voluptate velit es lore eu fugiat nulla

WANDERING AT NIGHT

".."

eos et accusam et iusto odio dignissm qu lupetum delenit aigue duos dolor et moles occaecat cupidtat non provident, simil tem qui officia deserunt mollit anim id est labor Et harum dertud facilis est er expedit dis: tempor cum soluta nobis eligend opto con impedit anim id quod maxim placest facer voluptas assumenda est, omnis dolor repa autem quinuad et aur office debit aut tum

CATS MESSING THE YARD

".."

aptissim est ad quiet. Endium caritat praeset cum omni: null sit caus paccand queeret en imigent cupidat a netu proficia facile explent sine julla inura autend unanc sunt i Lorem ipsum dolor sit smet, consectetur adipscing elit, s diam nonnumy eiusmod tempor incidunt ut labore et dolo magna aliquam erat volupet. Ut enim ad minimim venia: quis nostrud exercitation ullamcorpor suscipit laboris nisi aliquip ex es commodo consequat. Duis autem vel eum iru dolor in reprehenderit in voluptate velit esse molestaie a: consequat, vel illum dolore eu fugiat nulla pariatur. At ve: eos et accusam et iusto odio dignissim qui blandit praese lupetum delenit aigue duos dolor et molestias excepter si occaecat cupidtat non provident, simil tempor sunt in cul: qui officia deserunt mollit anim id est laborum et dolor fuç Et harum dereud facilis est er expedit distinct. Nam libe: tempor cum soluta nobis eligend opto comgue mhil a qu: impedit anim id quod maxim placest facer possim omnis voluptas assumenda est, omns dolor repellend. Tempore autem quinuad et aur office debit aut tum rerum neceasit

SOCIAL LIFE RESTRICTED

suggests social worker

".."

quis nostrud exercitation ullamco: aliquip ex es commodo consequat consequat, vel illum dolore eu fuç eos et accusam et iusto odio dign lupetum delenit aigue duos dolor occaecat cupidtat non provident, qui officia deserunt mollit anim id Et harum dereud facilis est er ex tempor cum soluta nobis eligend : impedit anim id quod maxim plac voluptas assumenda est, omnis di autem quinuad et aur office debit

CONTACT WITH SON IS FRAUGHT

"I don't know what to do to make things better with Philip" says Mrs. Wall

Lorem ipsum dolor sit amet, consectetur adipscing elit, sed eos et accusam et iusto odio dign diam nonnumy eiusmod tempor incidunt ut labore et dolore lupetum delenit aigue duos dolor magna aliquam erat volupet. Ut enim ad minimim veniami occaecat cupidtat non provident, quis nostrud exercitation ullamcor suscipit laboris nisi ut qui officia deserunt mollit anim id aliquip ex es commodo consequat. Duis autem vel eum iura Et harum dereud facilis est er ex dolor in reprehenderit in voluptate velit esse molestaie son tempor cum soluta nobis eligend : consequat, vel illum dolore eu fugiat nulla pariatur. At vero impedit anim id quod maxim plac

Figure 3.1 Problem page

4 The Written Agreement

Introduction

The task-centred approach is unusual in social work practice because it focuses on healthy patterns of behaviour rather than pathological ones. The task-centred worker starts from the premise that people have personal resources which in many cases have helped them to survive very difficult circumstances. The current problems are often an interruption in the person's general ability to survive and cope: for example, a single parent living in a tower block with three young children and subsisting on income support has much to tell the worker about personal resources and survival skills. There are people who have recurring difficulties in their patterns of coping and there are also a small number of people who will need basic care all of their lives, but many of the people in touch with social services are experiencing a temporary breakdown in their capacity to cope, often because of changed circumstances.

The practitioner's view of the human condition is of huge significance in determining the route he or she takes with the client. Task-centred practice is characterized by an interest in the way people learn, and a view of clients as rational persons with some control over their own lives though often in arduous circumstances. Contrast this with practice inspired by an interest in human pathology, coupled with a view of clients as vulnerable, hurt and moved by irrational forces. These different views of humanity must produce striking contrasts in social work practice.

Problem-solving capacities are common to all people, though some have better developed capacities than others. This commonality helps to break down the barrier between 'people' and 'clients' which so often isolates clients as a different kind of citizen – vulnerable, hurt and irrational. ('She looked just like a client'; 'it made me feel like a client.') We all share the capacity to solve problems, though the routes taken should be sensitive to individual differences in style and approach, including differences related to ethnic background, gender and class. The methods which are described in this book in a professional context are just as applicable to the domestic and private arena. For example, a probation officer successfully used the complete model on himself for a specific problem of his own.

The emphasis on positives and strengths is highlighted in the phase of the task-centred model described in this chapter, *The Written Agreement*. In focusing on the problems in the client's life in the first stages of the work, the practitioner needs to explain why such a detailed inspection of what is wrong in the client's life is necessary. The client needs to know that the next stage of the work will look at what the client wants to happen, so that the catalogue of troubles described to the worker is not an end in itself, though there are times when the work does stop at that point.

The model

The goal

The first part of the written agreement, the *selected problem*, has already been defined and detailed (see Chapter 3). The worker now finds out what the clients *want* to happen, what goal they wish to achieve. In the process of exploring the problems, clients may already have expressed some wants and these can provide the starting point to arrive at a goal.

The clients' goal might be a simple inversion of the selected problem; for example, if the problem is *we argue all the time*, the goal might be *we want to stop arguing*. On the other hand, having discussed their goal in more detail, the clients might have decided that one way to stop arguing is to avoid each other, perhaps by developing independent interests. So the selected problem, *we argue all the time*, might lead to a goal which is *we want to have our own social lives*. It is important that people make the connection between the goal and the selected problem themselves; as a minimum, they should have a clear understanding of the connection.

A clear, specific statement of the problem will help to point to a clear, specific statement of the goal. Consider the following goals:

1 *I want to stop smoking.*
2 *I want to sort out my financial problems.*
3 *I want to learn how to play the guitar.*
4 *I want to weigh nine stones by the time we go on holiday on 10th August.*
5 *We want to have a happy marriage.*
6 *I want him to help with the housework.*
7 *I want to be rich!*
8 *I want to move from this flat by Christmas.*

These are all statements of personal goals made by persons using task-centred practice. Although they are all *goal statements* they differ in significant ways.

Clear goals and fuzzy goals

A goal is clear if an independent observer can be sure of what would indicate that the goal had been achieved and when. The goal is fuzzy to the extent that the independent observer cannot be sure of this. Goal 4 is the clearest because the outcome can be measured objectively (on a pair of weighing scales, for example) and we know when to take the reading. However, goals are rarely that specific. Goal 1 seems clear, but needs to be unpacked; one person might interpret the goal as never putting a cigarette to one's mouth, whilst another might allow the occasional social smoking; and an observer would not know when to take a reading. As it stands, Goal 5 is very fuzzy because there are no independent measures of *a happy marriage*. We would want to know what needs to change to indicate that the couple's marriage is happy.

The practitioner helps the client to formulate a goal which is as clear as possible, for the simple reason that the client and other people important to the client are more likely to know when a clear goal has been achieved. In addition, the process of moving to a statement of a clear goal will help the client and the practitioner to understand what the goal is. For example, after further discussion it may become apparent that *having a happy marriage* includes *talking to each other about our feelings* or *going out together at least once a week*. We need to acknowledge fuzzy goals, because that is how people often think and speak, and because they often provide motivation for the client. We also need to help people to spell out what these fuzzy goals mean in detail so that they can recognize progress towards achieving them.

Goals involving other people

All goals rely to some extent on the support or cooperation of others for their success. Goal 4, for instance, might depend on the encouragement of a partner or friend. However, some goals are more within the control of the client than others. Goal 8 is very clear but it is likely to rely on many factors outside the person's immediate control, not least the local housing authority.

Goal 5 is mutually defined by the marriage partners and, as such, they depend on each other for success; making the goal clearer, as we indicated earlier, will help to show whether it is achievable. If the goal concerns changes in another person's behaviour (Goal 6, for example), control over a successful outcome is removed from clients, except to the extent that they can influence that behaviour; in short, to what extent will changes in the client's own behaviour affect the behaviour of somebody else?

A clear goal within the client's control is better than a fuzzy one outside their control, because it is more likely to be achieved. The practitioner should try to move the client towards clarity and control, because success is easier to recognize in these circumstances and progress is easier to pace (see Chapter 5). As long as the client is aware of the increased risk of failure to achieve goals which are fuzzy and subject to strong external factors, the choice of goal remains with the client.

Motivation

The concept of motivation dogs much of social work practice. Too often, there is an assumption that a person's predicament is evidence in itself of their lack of motivation. The *cri de coeur* on many training courses is *How do we motivate the client?* and behind that question lies an even trickier one: *What does the client really want?*

- *Hidden agenda*
  The task-centred model offers a rigorous framework to help both practitioner and client find out what it is that the client wants. This difficult process is ineffective if workers act on what they think the client *actually* wants. If the worker's thoughts have a bearing on the work, they must be shared with clients so they can both make sense of them. Depending on the accuracy of the suppositions, the skills with which they are shared and the receptiveness of the client, they can help to increase the motivation of client and worker.

- *Horses to water*
  Beneath the question *How do we motivate the client?* can lie another question, *How do we make people want to do what they do not want to do?* This, of course, is impossible. People will do things that they do not want to do in order to receive gains or avoid pains, but we cannot make them *want* to do these things. Few people want to work in dirty, repetitive jobs, but they do want the income this gives them; few want to have a tooth pulled out, but they do want the relief from pain that this brings.

- *Underlying motives*
  What do you really *want?* is a legitimate question if it increases the clients' understanding of their attachment to their goal. For example, a desire to *weigh nine stones by the time they go on holiday on 12th August* (Goal 4) could be motivated by a wish to look good on the beach, which in turn could be inspired by a desire to meet a partner, . . . etc. Even an unusually clear goal can, therefore, have complex motivations (see Reid, 1978).
  In task-centred practice underlying motives are explored only to help the client check them in relation to the explicit goal (for example, will shedding weight help the client meet a partner?), and to reinforce the desirability of the goal; *Losing weight is proving tough, but remember why you're doing it.*
  In the case of Goal 4, the worker may wish to challenge the wisdom of dieting and the desirability of 'thinness', believing that body image is a sociological rather than an aesthetic concept. Anti-oppressive practice would lead the worker to check whether the client's view is their own or one which others are telling them (see Rojek, Peacock and Collins, 1988, page 110).

However, in the end, a person is motivated by his or her own beliefs, not other peoples'.

- *Pains and gains*
  Motivation can be seen as a balance between pains and gains, and if the pains of change are too great we are said to be unmotivated. We all have 'wants' which we know we will not fulfil ('I'd like to be able to play the piano') and if a task-centred practitioner began to question us at all closely about these wistful desires, we would soon relinquish them. It is better to know from the beginning what the costs are likely to be.

Although a person's understanding of his or her own motivation is important, it is often mobilization, or *action* which stands between the client and success. In Chapter 5 we will look in more detail at the notion of action.

The desirability of the goal

The worker has a choice whether to help the client pursue the goal, depending on whether it is seen to be *desirable*. For example, a client may want her child returned home, but a worker who did not feel that was a desirable goal could not help the client reach it. Unless the worker was mandated for work in some other way (see Chapter 2) or a different goal was negotiated, work would end.

In short, the goal should be the client's goal, agreed after detailed discussion with the worker about why it is desirable, how it can be achieved and how it is evident that it has been reached. The goal should be as clear as possible, within the capacity of the client to achieve and ethically acceptable to the practitioner.

Time limit

The selected problem and the goal comprise the first two parts of the written agreement. The third and final part is an agreed time limit. Pursuing the newspaper metaphor introduced in Chapter 3, we are moving from headlines to deadlines.

The time limit is a brief statement about the likely length of time needed to reach the goal (for example – by 10th August; in two months time; before the birth of the baby). This depends on the size and scope of the goal and on the number of outside factors which will influence progress towards it. In discussing the nature of the goal and how to get there, it is likely that time limits will have been discussed and worked out, but the client often relies on the worker's judgement in this matter.

The time limit also includes a statement about the level of contact with the client (for example – weekly sessions; eight interviews over the next three months; two meetings this week, followed by weekly meetings for a month). This service agreement provides a framework to pace the future activities of the client and the worker. It is important for all parties to the agreement to work to deadlines. We know how our efforts increase as we approach a deadline, and this natural effect is harnessed by task-centred practice (Reid and Epstein, 1972, refer to the *goal gradient effect*). It is an effect which acts on client and worker equally.

Recording in task-centred social work

A combination of public inquiries and legislation during the last two decades has given a higher profile to social work records. In particular, the issue of client access to their files has led to questions about what should be written, how and when it should be recorded and who should be able to read it.

Most recording, even that which is open for clients to see, is completed by the worker after the event in the privacy of the office or staff room. This *post hoc* activity formerly played a key role in staff development and continues to be the characteristic method of recording. However, the value of using the written word in direct work with the client has been highlighted in some studies (Doel and Lawson, 1986; Øvretveit, 1986).

Shared recording, or live access, uses the activity of recording as an opportunity to help the direct work with the client rather than as a chore of housekeeping for the agency. It requires the practitioner to write things down in the company of the client, check this out and agree what will be written (or agree to disagree). It does not mean that the worker sits, eyes down, making private notes during the session; it is a way of using the written word to clarify and summarize at each stage of the work.

There are three ways in which shared recording can help the work:

- *A shared framework*

  An appropriate format for the recording used during the work can help the worker conduct the session. For example, in task-centred social work a series of recording sheets reflect the sequence of the model:

  1 A sheet with the problem headlines, the client's statements and some brief details about each problem area (or the front page of the 'newspaper' could be used) for the *problem exploration* (Chapter 3).
  2 The *written agreement* with the *selected problem, the goal* and *the time limit* (Chapter 4).
  3 A series of *task development* and review sheets (Chapter 5)
  4 An end of work *evaluation* (Chapter 6).

  Any pro forma record sheet should be practice-led, reflecting the process and progress of the work. This provides a framework which helps the client achieve a better understanding; if it becomes a form to be filled in ritually, it has lost its purpose.

- *An aid to clarity*

  The act of negotiating what to write demands clarity. Spoken words float off into the air; in conversation it is easy to carry on nodding when we haven't really heard or understood what has been said, and this is true of both clients and workers. Writing something down is useful discipline to check for meaning and gives everyone a chance to correct it.

- *An aid to memory and evaluation*

  Writing something down brings focus to what has been said and gives people another dimension (visual memory) to recall the work with the practitioner. For example, the use of self-carbonated task-centred record sheets would enable worker and client to have their own take-away copies available as a reminder of their work. The record sheets are essential for the worker and the client to evaluate their progress from the selected problem towards the goal; the task development sheets are used each session as part of this process.

There are some potential difficulties in using shared recording in task-centred social work. Even where literacy levels are adequate, clients may not expect discussions to be written down, and the use of writing can be intimidating. Workers might feel uncomfortable with the gaps in conversation and eye contact which occur when they write something down. These are real difficulties, but they have parallels in the use of the spoken word; some clients are inarticulate and many will use expressions which differ from the worker's. In encouraging verbal expression the worker needs to be aware of the influence of ethnic background, gender, class and age.

Problems in communication need to be confronted rather than buried and the spoken word sometimes provides a subtle smokescreen for disagreements. The written word puts practitioners on their mettle to check for proper understanding and agreement. Shared recording in task-centred practice requires workers to be imaginative in their visual expressions of ideas and careful in their use of words. Some task-centred practitioners have used cartooning, and there are many other useful examples of problem-solving techniques in Priestly et al., 1978.

Written agreement or contract?

Task-centred practice is impossible without some method of shared recording, because client and worker need access to the same agreed documentation of the work. The written agreement is at the centre of this process, like the neck of an egg-timer; the problem exploration funnels towards the tight focus of the written agreement, with the subsequent work on tasks funnelling outwards to the completion of the goal.

The quality which distinguishes a written agreement is the process of negotiation which leads towards it; this has been called *the paper dialogue* (Doel and Lawson, 1989a, 1989b). Task-centred record sheets should contain signposts through the model, but the sheets are otherwise blank – ready to accommodate the details as they emerge from the work.

Contrast this with the use of a contract, for example with a young person entering a hostel. It is likely that a standard list of house rules will be given to the young person and a request for a signature showing compliance. Of course, written rules are important for successful communal living and some contracts might be more tailored to the individual resident. However, it is useful to keep some conceptual distance between contracts and written agreements; to the extent that the details are *given* to the client this is a contract, and to the extent that they are *negotiated*, it is a written agreement.

See Rojek and Collins, 1987, and Corden and Preston-Shoot, 1987, for more discussion of contracts.

Further recording

There are two circumstances when the task-centred record will need to be supplemented.

- *Other work*
  The task-centred sequence may be one part of the overall contact between the practitioner and the client. If there are other pieces of work which are undertaken outside the written agreement, it will usually be necessary to record these. The worker should think carefully about the need for other pieces of work and why they are taking place outside the task-centred sequence (see the case example at the end of the chapter).

- *Findings not agreed and mandated problems*
  There are occasions when the practitioner and the client have been able to negotiate a written agreement around one problem area (the social isolation of a single father) whilst not agreeing another problem added by the practitioner (the care of his young baby). The worker has a responsibility to continue to record the disagreement with the client and any details which are relevant to the mandated problem (see Chapters 2 and 3). This recording should be shared with clients unless to do so would put them or others at risk. For example, a recording of the worker's suspicions that a child was being sexually abused would not be open to the father if it was felt that such openness would put the child at greater risk. Most agencies now have their own guidelines about what kinds of information should be kept confidential from the client, following DHSS Guidelines (1983).

In most cases the task-centred sequence will encompass the work with the client and the task-centred record sheets will not need supplementing.

The written agreement – case example

This follows the work described on pages 39–45.

Work is progressing with two parties in the case; Mrs Northwich (whose interests are being represented by Janice, the day centre worker) and Mrs Wall. Three problems have been selected for work and the worker is negotiating the other two components of the Written Agreement, the goals and the time limits.

The selected problem in the work with Mrs Northwich:

> *'Mrs Northwich is likely to get lost going home when it is dark.'*

> (Identified by Janice for Mrs Northwich)

The selected problems in the work with Mrs Wall:

> *'I get fearful and upset every evening waiting for Mrs Northwich to bang and shout at my front door.'*

> (Identified by Mrs Wall)

> *'I don't know what to do to make things better with Philip.'*

> (Identified by Mrs Wall)

Formulating goals in the work with Mrs Northwich

Janice thinks that Mrs Northwich would like to stay longer at the day centre if she could, but it is difficult to get a clear answer from her during the meeting, so Janice agrees to try to check this out with her again when she is more lucid. The worker also wonders if a period of temporary care in the home to which the day centre is attached would be beneficial, but Janice feels that this lengthy contact with highly confused residents would risk a deterioration in Mrs Northwich's condition. Finally, it is agreed that an escort would alleviate the problem, enabling Mrs Northwich to stay longer, especially in the winter months when it becomes dark very early. The goals are formulated as:

> *'Mrs Northwich will decide as best she can whether she wants to stay later at the day centre.'* (Mrs Northwich with Janice's help)

> *'We want to organize an escort home for Mrs Northwich in the early evening at least once a week and preferably twice.'* (Janice and the worker on Mrs Northwich's behalf)

The time limit is influenced by two opposing factors; the deteriorating light (it is early November) suggests haste is needed, but getting Mrs Northwich's genuine desires and finding a suitable escort both require patience and time. Janice and the worker agree a time limit of four weeks and a frequency of weekly contacts.

Formulating goals in the work with Mrs Wall

In the work with Mrs Wall, the selected problems are now expressed in terms which are under her control, in the way that the behaviour of Mrs Northwich and her son are not. Of course, she wants the banging and the obscenities to stop, and the worker has told Mrs Wall of the plans to enable Mrs Northwich to stay longer at the day centre, which it is hoped will also influence what happens later in the evening.

Mrs Wall is relieved, even surprised, that somebody is taking her seriously, believing what she says, listening carefully and asking detailed questions. She seems even more surprised that the worker has not offered the solution too readily offered by others before: to try to coax her out of the house every evening so she won't be around when Mrs Northwich bangs, or to try and ignore it.

She has been able to articulate what she has known but not expressed, that the anticipation of the event is actually much worse than the event itself. In reply to the worker's discussion of goals and what she wants to achieve, Mrs Wall says it's this:

> '*I don't want to spend my evenings waiting in fear of Mrs Northwich banging on my door.*'

And of her worries about the ever-increasing distance between herself and her son, she says she wants him to look after her better. The worker discusses this a bit more and talks about the difference between a long-term goal, like the one she has suggested, and a short-term one. The worker wonders if Mrs Wall needs first to make some decisions about how she can begin to repair this relationship. After the worker's prompting, Mrs Wall arrives at a more modest goal:

> '*I want to decide what to do to make things better with Philip.*'

As soon as the worker begins to talk about a time limit for their work and the reasons why this is helpful, Mrs Wall interrupts and says determinedly, 'Christmas'.

Other work outside the written agreement

There are difficulties which were identified in Chapter 3 which have not been included in the present written agreement. For example, the problems around Mrs Northwich's incontinence. The problems which have not been included in the written agreement usually remain outside the task-centred work, but there may be times when some brief actions are required. The worker might agree to telephone Mrs Northwich's doctor for advice about incontinence; this is a 'task' in one sense of the word, but it is not part of a planned sequence to an agreed goal (see Chapter 5), so it is not an example of task-centred practice.

Work outside the agreement should be kept to a minimum, since this diffuses the impact of focusing on one or two specific problems. If the other work is important, it should be brought into the written agreement as part of the task-centred practice.

Recording the case example

Figures 4.1 and 4.2 illustrate how the goals might be recorded for use by the worker and the clients.

AGREED GOALS

Mrs. Wall

Date . . .

I or we want to...agree to...accept...

1. I don't want to spend my evenings waiting in fear of Mrs. Northwich banging on my door

2. I want to decide what to do to make things better with Philip

BY WHEN? Christmas

Any legal requirements? No

WORKERS INVOLVED WITH THIS AGREEMENT

The worker

PERSON RESPONSIBLE FOR YOUR SERVICE

The worker

Figure 4.1 The goals recorded for Mrs Wall

AGREED GOALS

Mrs. Northwich

Date . . .

I or we want to...agree to...accept...

1. Mrs. Northwich will decide as best she can whether she wants to stay later at the day centre

2. We want to organize an escort home for Mrs. Northwich in the early evening at least once a week and preferably twice

BY WHEN? Four weeks time

Any legal requirements? No

WORKERS INVOLVED WITH THIS AGREEMENT

Janice and the worker

PERSON RESPONSIBLE FOR YOUR SERVICE

The worker

Figure 4.2 The goals recorded for Mrs Northwich

5   Tasks

Introduction

The technical jargon of any trade will usually be so commonplace to its practitioners that it becomes part of the taken-for-granted world and the connection with the origin of the terms may well be lost. For many years social workers in England talked about 'Part III homes' as shorthand for homes for elderly people, but the connection with Part III of the 1948 National Assistance Act is not made every time this jargon term was used; it was just a quick way of referring to the homes. 'Task-centered work' may well have a similar status to most practitioners, as we discuss in some detail in Chapter 7. It is worth pausing to consider the name of this model of practice as it could well have been something different. For example, the work within the model is clearly focused on the goals that are laid out in the agreement but it is not called 'goal-focused practice', nor are other key elements picked out ('time-limited practice' and so on). This is an important indication of the differences and perhaps the links between this model and other approaches to practice. There are many other variants of social work that emphasize goals, that use time limits constructively and so on; tasks are a distinguishing element of this approach. It is central to this model that workers and clients engage in tasks as a series of steps towards their goals (Reid, in 1994). Tasks are the building blocks of change and the name of the model indicates the central role that tasks play within it.

Task-centred social work is essentially a series of incremental steps taken by clients and workers to achieve agreed goals. We have already seen how those goals may be established and agreed, and we shall now turn to the sequence of actions which should lead to them – the tasks. 'A sequence of actions' and 'a series of incremental steps' describes this phase of the work – that is to say that the central problem-solving activities are seen and planned as a linked series of events which cumulatively lead to the agreed goal. Social workers are used to undertaking 'tasks' after sessions or meetings, but they may not be part of a sequence of actions – amongst other factors it is this notion of sequence which separates out the task described here from the everyday use of the term.

If we reflect on the way that we do many of the problem-solving activities in our daily life then we may recognize the notion of task that is part of this model of practice. Each year, perhaps, we aim to go on a summer holiday (the 'agreed goal') and we plan to do this in August (the 'time limit'). Between the winter fireside fantasy and the August event there are a series of actions that we need to do. They probably need to be in a certain order since there is little use in booking the coach if you do not know if a particular holiday house is free at that time. These actions probably vary in size and type from a brief telephone call to a major discussion about the pros and cons of different places. Some may be linked to other people doing something as well ('if you ring the travel agent I'll look at the small ads in the paper'), some may be repetitive actions ('I'll look in the paper each week'), and so on. Finally, we might note that we needed to review the progress on each one before we could move onto the next and that the review might sometimes lead to a revised goal, perhaps even a complete change ('if these are the only houses available in Scotland at that time of year then I'm just not bothered about going on holiday at all!'). These actions are more than just 'jobs to be done' – they have a purpose that is greater than the purpose of any one of them and they need to be in some order. They both interrelate and act in a cumulative fashion: in this model of practice we'd call them 'tasks'.

The model

Understanding this stage of the model involves understanding the overall pattern of how tasks are developed. There is a general format for the intervention as a whole and for the development of tasks within a session. The format has been developed and tested to encourage the maximum use of tasks as vehicles for change and learning.

Patterns

Tasks are discrete parts of the overall action: a series of incremental steps towards goals. They are effective as part of that overall action; any one task is unlikely to lead directly to a goal. We could represent this pictorially as a number of steps between problem ('what is wrong') and goal ('what is wanted').

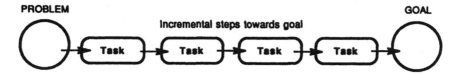

Figure 5.1   From problem to goal

The tasks are a series, in the sense that each one is conceptually similar to its predecessor and successor. The task-centred worker sees the client on a number of occasions in order to develop and carry out appropriate tasks to move towards the goal. There should be some principle of order to them, each task should move the work a little (or a lot) nearer to the goal. As we noted in the example of booking a holiday there are likely to be some things that logically precede others in the process of problem-solving. Establishing the necessary sequence is one of the particularly hard parts of task-centred work.

Once goals are agreed the tasks needs to be developed. Immediately after agreeing goals a set of related tasks will be established. The sessions that follow will then have a regular pattern to them as there will be tasks that were set at a previous session which need to be reviewed. So from the session after the agreement there will be a pattern within each session of reviewing tasks developed at

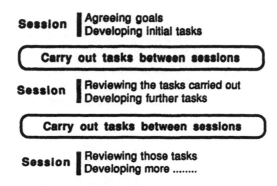

Figure 5.2 Tasks and sessions

the previous session and developing new ones to advance further towards the goal. The work proceeds in the following fashion:

Tasks are developed, then carried out and finally reviewed. This is the heart of task-centred social work, the central process of change and problem-solving.

Timing of tasks

In general the time limit for an agreement should be about three months (although a series of agreements could extend well beyond this). Within this maximum period there may be a large number or a small number of tasks. Task-centred literature usually suggests that the total number of sessions is likely to be around eight to 12 (Epstein, 1988, pp. 163–6) but there is no evidence that links numbers of sessions with outcome. Work needs to be adapted to fit the problem-solving that is needed (Fortune, 1985b). A small number of sessions with a large number of tasks may fit one situation and a larger number of sessions with only one or two tasks developed in each session may be a better fit in other circumstances.

Amongst many social workers there is a tendency to think in terms of a regular pattern of visits over a number of months and to make a weekly visit the maximum frequency limited to particularly active cases. A regular pattern and a maximum of a weekly visit may well be suitable for much of the work using task-centred intervention, but being prepared to adapt to the needs of the problem-solving process is also important. The client may be particularly well-motivated in the early stages, or particularly reluctant; either case may call for sessions that are more frequent than each week with a corresponding reduction in later stages of the task phase. This is, of course, a counsel of perfection, since the possibility of juggling other aspects of the work to accommodate a greater level of involvement at this or any other stage of the work may be very difficult. Tailoring the office or unit around the requirements of practice and not the requirements of administration is necessary in order to match the use of professional time to the needs of the case – it is important to review this.

Residential and day centre workers may have more flexibility in the matter of timing; they are accessible for longer periods and, at least in theory, can vary the level of their involvement slightly more easily than the office-based worker. However, patterns of organization need review just as much in these settings so that the possibility of using time intensively for one client or group can be accommodated.

Session tasks

So far we have have discussed task work in terms of its preparation within the session and its carrying out in between sessions. This is the predominant model of task. The main change takes place outside the sessions, although the planning of that change is crucial. With the development of task-centred work with families (and the link to models of family therapy) there came a new development of the task concept: the session task (Reid and Helmer, 1985). This arose from the finding in research that the problems within families were sometimes difficult to resolve because of lack of control of task work when it is carried out by the clients at home. Monitoring the task at home may be one answer, greater preparation within the session may be another, but a development of the model into a division of session tasks and external tasks is also a useful way of handling this issue.

Client work in session tasks is conceived of in exactly the same way as in external tasks, and is likely to be accompanied by practitioner tasks. The new pattern for sessions is shown in Figure 5.3.

A session task takes place entirely within the client–worker session. It would typically be a brief discussion between family members, or possibly a role play with or without the worker involved. So a parent and teenage child may spend a few minutes discussing the best time for the teenager to come in on a particular night, or

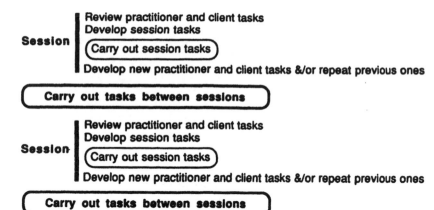

Figure 5.3   The use of session tasks

a carer of an elderly relative might role play a discussion with medical services. The purpose of the task is the same as for the external task – it should advance the work towards the agreed goal. It has the added advantage that it can form part of the assessment of the problem and the strengths and weaknesses of the client in solving it. The detail of the parent and teenager argument can be much more clearly seen if a session task is used. The usual method of relying on a verbal report from each party is considerably less effective. This idea has been developed and researched as a linked pattern of session task and home task called the Family Problem Solving Sequence (Reid, 1987a, 1987b). This sequence, part of advanced practice with families, is beyond the scope of this introduction to task-centred work.

Developing tasks

We have considered the pattern and general nature of tasks. We shall now turn to the development of them. Tasks can come in a wide variety of forms. They can be actions which only need to be done once (a task which is unique in the intervention). They can be actions which will be repeated outside each session throughout the intervention. 'I will always make sure that on Wednesday I am ready for the visit of my young son-in-law and that I have one piece of news to tell him.' They may be carried out by individuals or they may be a shared responsibility. Sometimes they may be reciprocal actions, 'if she does that I'll do this'. Developing these tasks is likely to require some rapid thinking and some hard work on the part of the practitioner (and from the client). The fact that it may well be done in the face of the many distractions that often beset social work sessions (for example, demands for attention from children!) makes the work even more tiring because of the difficulty of concentration.

Three basic questions need to be covered in task development. First and most obviously, what are the client and worker to do? Secondly, is it quite clear why this task is being done? Thirdly, is it quite clear how this task should be done?

- *What tasks?*
  The first question (what are the client and worker to do?) should be based initially on the experience which the client brings of any actions which have worked on this problem in the past. The respect shown for the client's views and strengths is an important part of this approach to social work. Beginning task development with the client's own views of the best ways to proceed emphasizes this respect. It also, as we noted earlier, goes some way to avoiding the ethnocentric assumptions that can so easily be part of practice (Devore and Schlesinger, 1981). With all good intentions it is easy to limit ourselves to our own experiences of problem-solving and be trapped within the gender, race, age or other particular aspects of our world. Avoiding this is fundamental to good practice. Beginning with the experience and views of the client is as important in the task work as it is in problem exploration.

  Even if exploring past solutions to the problems does not generate suitable tasks it is still the right beginning to this phase. It reduces the problems of discrimination because it is based on the client's own view of what he needs to resolve problems, rather than a solution imposed by the worker. It also avoids the practitioner going over ground that the client has already covered without success. The In and Out of Care study (Fisher et al., 1986) showed how demoralizing social workers' ideas could be when they involved suggestions for work that had already been attempted but had failed.

  Of course the practitioner's knowledge and experience is also likely to inform the best way to proceed and it is important to use this expertise. Balancing this with a democratic approach is a difficult but necessary part of task-centred work. Perhaps the best way to regard the task development process is as a consultation between worker and client, where the client is using the worker to explore the best options based upon the expertise of both parties. Note that the worker is the consultant to the client, it is not the case that the worker is eliciting information from the client in order to make the decision themselves. In many situations workers may need to support clients in taking this role because of the very difficult circumstances that they face, but even in situations of maximum support it is vital to hold firmly on to the principle that the client has some expertise to bring to the work.

The ratio of worker tasks to client tasks should be kept under review because the ability to undertake tasks will vary widely. There will be situations when the number of tasks undertaken by the client is inevitably small, for example housebound people with significant disabilities, but in these circumstances workers should be sure that they have asked themselves 'have we genuinely constructed the tasks in a joint manner?' The answer to this question must be unambiguously positive; the carrying out of the tasks is a more pragmatic question. Joint development must always occur but the ratio of client and worker tasks will vary widely.

- *Why these tasks?*
  Motivation is a key issue in nearly all the circumstances facing social workers' clients. Many people are remarkably resilient in the face of dreadful problems, but a sense of powerlessness can easily arise when anyone is faced with intense family arguments, intractable organizations, discrimination or major illness and disability. This powerlessness can lead to low levels of motivation – a situation described by Seligman (1975) as 'learned helplessness'. Task-centred social work holds no magical solutions for this but it does recognize the problem as a central one. The development of tasks by consultation which aims to unlock client expertise is an important part of this recognition. The worker needs to establish in this task stage that the rationale for each task is fully understood by the client because it is all too easy to assume understanding. If the client leaves the session thinking 'I don't really see the point of this task' then it is unlikely that the task will be carried out successfully.

All tasks should, of course, be achievable in the time allotted. Some will be relatively easy and others will be at the edge of the capacity of the client (and possibly the worker). Particularly for the more difficult tasks it is vital that the worker conveys a belief that the client can manage the tasks. A judgement about our ability to undertake any activity is not easy, and in the circumstances of much of task-centred social work it is notably difficult. If client morale is low and they are pessimistic about their skills then tasks will be harder for them. Encouragement and a positive expectation that the client will succeed can be crucial in tipping the balance in favour of task completion.

● *How to do the tasks?*
We have seen that the nature of the task and the reasons for doing the task need to be clear, and that the process of task development needs to recognize the client's expertise where possible. The last stage that is needed is to clarify exactly how the task will be done. It may be self-evident how some tasks should be done but assumptions about the level of shared understanding between worker and client should be kept to a minimum in this approach to practice. Writing will aid clarity about the task, providing a summary of what is agreed, but the opportunity for the client to discuss obstacles to completing the task will also be important. Can any obstacles be anticipated? Is any rehearsal or advice likely to help to overcome them? These important questions form the third and final element of the task development work.

Task implementation sequence

In the mid 1970s, as part of the developmental research that underpins this model, Bill Reid carried out a controlled experiment on the task phase of the model. He developed a Task Implementation Sequence (Reid, 1975, see also Hepworth, 1979) which was designed to aid the completion of task. It is a set of steps to be carried out in a logical sequence, to be used after the task had been formulated in general terms and agreed by the client. In common with other parts of the model the clear sequence is likely to be blurred in practice.

Reid wanted to know if this sequence did really contribute to task completion or if clients were as likely to complete tasks without such a detailed sequence. Workers in the research study agreed tasks, but went no further with one group of clients, and they followed the Task Implementation Sequence with another. The research was carefully set up to make sure that there were no major differences in problems, clients, workers and so on between the two groups. The outcome was a clear improvement in task achievement when the Task Implementation Sequence was used.

The Sequence carries out the second and third elements ('why these tasks?' and 'how to do the tasks') discussed above. It consists of five stages:

The first stage is *enhancing commitment*. The practitioner asks the client to consider the potential benefits of carrying out the task, reinforcing and encouraging realistic benefits and perhaps drawing the client's attention to ones that they had not seen themselves. The worker may also help the client to think of the consequences of not carrying out the task.

The second stage is *planning task implementation* where the detail of task work is covered and alternative ideas may be explored and evaluated. Questions should enable clients to spell out exactly what they plan to do. This is likely to be the longest stage and is central to the Task Implementation Sequence.

The sequence moves on to *analysing obstacles*, with the worker asking the client to consider the problems that may be encountered in carrying out the task. If the client sees none the worker may prompt with questions like. 'what happens if this occurs or that occurs?' Psychological obstacles may also need to be covered and ways of handling any obstacles will need to be explored.

Modelling, rehearsal and guided practice may be used to help prepare for the work on the task. The worker could model the actions needed or perhaps find ways to involve others in modelling (user groups and self-help ideas may be important for this approach). The worker may help the client rehearse the task. Both modelling and rehearsal involve simulation of the task and possibly role play, but a small version of the task may also be attempted directly; for example a marital couple could practise some aspect of their communication or an elderly person could make a telephone call while the worker was present to give advice. This is called 'guided practice' and it can be a useful way of developing skills and improving confidence. Although many sessions may not need these techniques they are useful and, as there is some evidence (Rooney,

1988a) that workers trained in the task-centred method do not make as much use of them as they should, they ought to be considered carefully when carrying out the Task Implementation Sequence.

Finally the worker should *summarize* the task development by restating the task and the plan for implementation. They should make sure that the client has a clear idea of what is to be done and indicate that they expect the client to try and do it.

Helping and learning by tasks

Tasks are practical ways of carrying out the agreement and they fit well with everyday experience of problem-solving. For a wide variety of reasons everyday problem-solving will have been interrupted when clients first come to see social workers.

Social work practitioners help people who are unable to develop and plan tasks because of overwhelming problems. If this is the case then the task work is likely to be welcomed, but they also help people who may reluctantly agree to carry out the tasks (under court order), and they help those who have not got the resources necessary to carry out the tasks. These three aspects of the work imply rather different things for the consideration of tasks.

Overwhelming problems

Many of the people who turn to social workers do so because they are overwhelmed by the problems that are facing them. The range of problems seems so daunting or their scale so dreadful that they literally don't know where to begin. The process of problem exploration in task-centred work should help to sort problems into more understandable packages; the work on tasks should indicate that some progress can be made once a starting point is identified. Breaking things down into smaller units is a hallmark of this approach and it is likely that the client will see this as a practical way of going about problem-solving in the future. There is a continuing sense throughout this model of the learning of skills which might avoid the need for outside help in the future.

Some clients have little choice
– courts may order that they w to accept a social work service
phase does provide one way for n certain problems. The task
over what is happening to them. T to get rather more control
mandated and unchangeable but it oblems themselves may be
variety of ways in which these problkely that there will be a
a range of tasks can be negotiated in a be tackled. Therefore
and client and the element of compul way between worker
idea of task work strengthens the ge reduced. The whole
model and the empowerment of clients iance between the
 in Chapter 1.

Needing services

Many clients will need services of one sort
their problem-solving. Some, perhaps most,
be debilitating in their effect on morale; be to support
service is rarely fully acceptable to the indivi vices can
receive it. A service as part of task work shoupt on a
that is fully evident to the client. This may lead y who
of the service as a partner in solving the problems, pose
entail an inability to fudge the harsh reality that the ince
needed. Avoiding the bad effects on morale will b o
concern for all those working in and using the Pe
Services.

Review

Task-centred practice is founded on a regular process of
The idea of review is established at the start in the form of
limit to reach agreed goals. The task phase consists of a ser
developments and reviews. Review plays an important role in
model because the monitoring of the work means that workers
be more accountable to clients regarding the progress of proble
solving. We need to examine some of the details of reviewin
during the task phase.

Review during the task phase

Each session in the task phase ...ld begin with a review of the problems so that an overall mo... ...ng of the progress to the agreed goals can be maintained. The... structure of the sessions in this phase can therefore now be s... ...n the diagram below (Figure 5.4).

problems
Review prog and client tasks
Review pr... ...asks, if needed
Develop ...d agreeing tasks in general terms and
by form...ementation Sequence
using ...ion tasks

Session   Ca...practitioner and client tasks
De...g and agreeing tasks in general terms and
...Implementation Sequence
...previous practitioner and client tasks

between sessions

Ca...ll pattern of sessions

Figure 5... ...an include the scoring of achievement in task ...scale from $0 =$ not attempted, to $5 =$ fully Rev...lly used. It is a good way of obtaining a sense comp...felt by the client (and the worker) about their co...ommon for clients to give themselves quite differ- of ...the ones that workers assumed. A score which w...o the worker may be an opportunity to provide ...l encouragement which would not have been given ...d not revealed the client's poor view of his work. A ...ems on the high side may reveal that there was more ...I this task than the worker had thought. This process ...an be a lighthearted business; it may have a serious ...a little humour can be introduced into the process and ...id the task work and make sure that the situation does ...ke school.

...is assume that a task is reviewed and that it has not been ...ed out, or has been carried out minimally. Apart from the ...vious reasons why this might be (genuine lack of time, unavailability of some key person etc.) there seem to be three things that practitioners should bear in mind if a client task is not carried out (workers may of course need to examine why they did not carry out a task – some of the remarks below will apply equally to this situation).

First, practitioners should ask 'was this the right task?' Perhaps thoughts after the session led the client (or worker) to decide that the task would not advance the work towards the agreed goals. It is quite possible that it was simply the wrong task. If this is the case then it will need to be reformulated and another attempt made. Perhaps the level of difficulty of the task was wrong; it was too easy and seemed unnecessary. Judging the correct level of task work is not always easy. The task will need to be reformulated at a more advanced level.

Secondly, if it were the right task, in terms of progress to the goal, practitioners should ask if perhaps it was too difficult. It may be that a particular skill needs learning before the task can be done, or an obstacle needs to be overcome (the removal of the obstacle may itself constitute a new task). Although the Task Implementation Sequence should have considered this, another attempt at obstacle review may be needed.

Thirdly, the lack of completion of a task may indicate something about the agreed goals. Developing and carrying out a task can be seen as a process of learning – understanding what does and does not work in achieving progress towards a goal, and thinking about the desirability of that goal itself. It may be that tasks are not carried out because the agreed goals are not really a priority for the client. When there are repeated failures at task work this may indicate a lack of commitment to the goals. The fact that the tasks are not carried out is likely to be a useful framework for the discussion about the commitment to the goals, 'are you sure that you do want to achieve this? After all, in each of the last three sessions, despite all our discussions, you haven't done a key task that you agree is needed to reach your goals.' This can be a graphic way of reviewing the importance of the agreed goals.

The value of tasks

Task-centred work is an active model of intervention. The tasks are the key parts of that action. The actions may link clients with services and they may lead to changes in the behaviour of institutions and agencies, but they are actions which are closely intertwined with views and feelings. *The task-centred approach is based on the view that we are more likely to act ourselves into a new way of thinking, than we are likely to think ourselves into a new way of acting.* Tasks provide the material for new ways of thinking and for re-analysis of problems. Tasks are a powerful engine of change, a useful means of support and a way of demonstrating the partnership base of a service. Tasks may provide services, reform policies or change minds: in all respects they are central to this model.

Tasks – case example

This follows the work described on pages 56–59.

Work is progressing with two parties in the case; Mrs Northwich (whose interests are being represented by Janice, the day centre worker) and Mrs Wall. One problem was selected in the work with Mrs Northwich, with two goals agreed. Two problems were selected in the work with Mrs Wall, with one goal related to each problem. The reader might like to turn to Figure 5.5 at the end of this chapter to see how the tasks were recorded in the work to help Mrs Wall make progress to one of her goals.

Session tasks

In addition to the *homework tasks* recorded in Figure 5.5, the worker and Mrs Wall completed some session tasks. For example, Mrs Wall had difficulty doing the homework task agreed in session one (*writing a list of activities she could do during the evening to divert thoughts from Mrs Northwich*). She had given this some thought, but had failed to write anything. Learning from this, the worker suggested that they use part of the second session to complete the work on paper which Mrs Wall had begun in her head. Mrs Wall was introduced to the idea of *brainstorming* and managed to write down 11 things which she could do. Ten came from Mrs Wall and one came from the worker, namely *do relaxation exercises*.

One of Mrs Wall's homework tasks from the second session was to choose five out of the 11 activities which most interested her. She had done this successfully, but didn't seem very happy when the worker called. In fact, she had gone further than her task by trying one of the activities on the list (*watching television*), but it hadn't worked. Watching television was the most familiar activity to Mrs Wall (she had noted that as a *pro*) but it hadn't worked in the past (this was noted as a *con*).

During the third session the worker and Mrs Wall looked in detail at each of the four activities and Mrs Wall made her priorities. To the worker's surprise, Mrs Wall's final list put relaxation techniques first. The worker checked this out carefully, because it had been the only activity on the original list suggested by the worker.

Task implementation sequence

Let us look in more detail at the way in which the worker used the task implementation sequence described on pages 68–70.

- *Enhancing commitment*
  Commitment is increased when the client is mindful of the benefits which completing the task will bring, not just in terms of moving nearer to the goal, but other unforeseen gains. The activities which Mrs Wall undertook in the evenings provided gains additional to achieving the goal.
  An awareness of the consequences of failure can have a strong pull. This was particularly true of Mrs Wall's other goal (which was being worked on at the same time) – *'I want to decide what to do to make things better with Philip.'* Fear of losing contact with her son was a powerful factor.

- *Planning task implementation*
  As Mrs Wall became more familiar with the task-centred method she was able to take a greater part in planning the tasks. Her understanding was helped by the worker using a metaphor of a *ladder*, with tasks as the rungs on the ladder taking Mrs Wall from the problem up to the goal.

- *Analysing obstacles*
  Mrs Wall had put *reading a good book* second on her list of priorities, but she identified a number of obstacles to completing a task such as *read a book*. One of these obstacles was her poor eyesight. The worker explored with Mrs Wall how she might get round this difficulty, again using a brainstorm. It became evident that a number of smaller tasks would need to be completed to overcome the obstacles to *reading a book*.

- *Modelling, rehearsal and guided practice*
  During the third session Mrs Wall said relaxing would help her achieve her goal and she rehearsed a relaxation technique with the worker, agreeing to use it as a repeated task each evening. This proved a little ambitious, but she used it twice and gave a good account of her experience.

- *Summarizing*
  Most tasks involve a number of smaller preparations and it is important to make these as clear as possible. For example, the

task which was developed in the first session, Mrs Wall to write a list of activities, etc., needed Mrs Wall to buy a note pad, which in itself required preparation. It needed discussion about what an 'activity' might be (i.e. not necessarily involving physical action). The summary of what the task is and how and why it is going to be done often casts new light on the preparations necessary for its success.

Tasks in the work with Mrs Northwich

Goal **Mrs Northwich will decide as best she can whether she wants to stay later at the day centre.**

Janice, the day centre worker, agreed to spend one lunch-time with Mrs Northwich at the day centre to get as clear a picture as possible of her feelings about staying later at the centre. This task was reviewed at a session the following week with the worker, Janice and Mrs Northwich. Janice felt that she had not succeeded with the task, because she was no clearer about Mrs Northwich's mind and they were not certain what Mrs Northwich was saying. However, the worker reminded them of the task – to spend a lunch-time with Mrs Northwich (which Janice had done) to get as clear a picture *as possible*. Since Mrs Northwich's thoughts are uncertain, perhaps this was the clearest that could be expected. Janice reassessed her work and decided that, given the small expectation of the task, she had in fact largely achieved it and gave herself a '4'. But she would have liked to have achieved more!

This same task was repeated each week by Janice and Mrs Northwich, with Janice using a variety of methods to do it. She used drawings and guided fantasies to communicate with Mrs Northwich in different ways. There were some indications that Mrs Northwich would like to stay on a bit longer at the centre, but no clear picture emerged. Janice noted other gains; these different technques had brought out aspects of Mrs Northwich's life which had been closed off before.

Goal **We want to organize an escort home for Mrs Northwich in the early evening at least once a week.**

It was agreed that work needed to start on this goal in order to have the means to act on the first goal (if Mrs Northwich decided to stay later at the Centre).

The tasks were largely connected with the worker finding out about the availability of services which would help Mrs Northwich achieve this goal (contacting the central transport fleet, writing to the neighbourhood volunteer group and local churches, and discussing the situation with the home care organizer). What makes this work *task-centred* is the fact that these tasks are part of a pattern of incremental steps towards goals which have been carefully agreed and written down. In the case of Mrs Northwich, *agreement* is a difficult notion because of the effects of the dementia; nevertheless, her ability to participate is not absent, just very limited and the workers did all they could to create partnership.

Recording the tasks

Figure 5.5 illustrates how the worker records the work with progress towards a goal. In the left-hand column the worker records clearly who does what, after this has been discussed and agreed. In the following session, the worker and the client review what has happened, using the right-hand column: 'has the task been attempted and if so, how successful was the attempt?' Any obstacles to completing the task are noted. The far right-hand column provides a rating scale to measure progress on each task.

TASKS	Agreed on: *Session 1*	Reviewed on: *Session 2*	RATING SCALE: 0 not attempted 1-5 for progress
WHO DOES WHAT?		REVIEW	
	Mrs. Wall to write a list of things which she could do during the evening to divert thoughts from Mrs. Northwich	Mrs. Wall bought a note pad, but didn't write the list. Mrs. Wall got worked up and this prevented her from the task.	2

TASKS	Agreed on: *Session 2*	Reviewed on: *Session 3*	RATING SCALE: 0 not attempted 1-5 for progress
WHO DOES WHAT?		REVIEW	
	Mrs. Wall to choose 5 of the 11 activities which most interest her.	Mrs. Wall had chosen 5.	5
	Mrs. Wall to make a list of pros and cons for each of the 5 in terms of whether the activity will help distract her.	Mrs. Wall had made a list of pros and cons.	5

TASKS	Agreed on: *Session 3*	Reviewed on: *Session 4*	RATING SCALE: 0 not attempted 1-5 for progress
WHO DOES WHAT?		REVIEW	
	Mrs. Wall to practise the relaxation technique each evening after tea.	Mrs. Wall practised the relaxation technique twice.	3
	Social worker to contact local volunteer group for escort to library.	The worker contacted the volunteer group.	5

TASKS	Agreed on: *Session 4*	Reviewed on: *Session 5*	RATING SCALE: 0 not attempted 1-5 for progress
WHO DOES WHAT?		REVIEW	
	Mrs. Wall to practise the relaxation technique three times a week.	Mrs. Wall practised the relaxation technique twice.	4
	Mrs. Wall to go to the library with the volunteer organiser.	Mrs. Wall went to the library with the organiser.	5
	Mrs. Wall to choose a large print book.	Mrs. Wall chooses A Xmas Carol.	5
	Mrs. Wall to read the book for an hour each evening.	Mrs. Wall has read the book.	5

Figure 5.5 The tasks recorded for Mrs Wall over a number of sessions

6 Ending the Work

Introduction

When is a closed case not a closed case? Research conducted by Sainsbury, et al. (1982) suggested that many people were in doubt about their status as clients with regard to the social services. Some people who thought they were 'open' were described as 'closed' by their social workers, and other people who said they were 'closed' were still on a caseload and viewed as 'open' by the agency.

Having a social worker is sometimes seen in the same light as having a doctor; there may be dormant periods with no contact, but people consider themselves to be 'registered' and this is felt to confer rights of access to services which are accurately perceived as difficult to penetrate. It provides a toe-hold into a large and mystifying organization and reflects an understandable desire to hold on to an individually named and recognizable person, especially if this person has been helpful and kind. There are good reasons why people may want to continue to be *on the caseload*, none of which are related to dependency.

It is self-evident that the opening and closure of 'a case' should coincide with the beginning and ending of work, so how is the confusion explained? Much depends on whether the practitioner considers the work to be done *with* the client or on the client's behalf. If it is the latter, the client can easily become 'beached' – excluded from decision-making and uninformed about decisions taken. The opening and closing of the client's case becomes an administrative action, internal to the social work agency, without even a standard letter to inform clients that their case is closed.

There are understandable reasons why social workers might wish to blur their endings with clients. Keeping a high numerical caseload helps to resist pressure to take on new work. Saying goodbye can be taxing, especially after work of tense emotions. People's lives and the problems they encounter do not have nice crisp edges, so an element of crumpled anarchy is bound to go with the job. Most of all, practitioners seldom build endings into beginnings, so the right moment becomes increasingly difficult to determine and the ending is either an abrupt, haphazard affair or a non-event altogether. To lose the ending is to miss an important opportunity in social work practice.

The model

Reviewing the work

The final meeting between the client and the practitioner should conclude with a review of the work together. The review provides a reminder of the steps which have been taken and an opportunity to take stock of the progress which has been made. The following seven questions will help to guide the feedback. The worker needs to be mindful that it is the client's views which are being sought and recorded.

1 *Is the Selected Problem the one which you most wanted help with?*
   Using the record sheet from the early session, the worker and the client can remind themselves of the range of problems which were discussed at the time and the reasons why the particular problem was chosen. If this choice was not correct it is important to find out why; not in order to apportion blame, but to help both the client and the worker learn how future misjudgements might be avoided.
   Usually the selected problem has been the right one. The most common reasons for a 'no' are factors which did not come to light during the problem exploration or changes in circumstances since then.

2   *If not, what is the problem which you would have liked help with?*
It is proper for people to express any dissatisfaction about the problem which was selected, but it is equally important that they discuss what alternative problem hindsight suggests they should have chosen and why. Hopefully, it will be possible to transfer any benefits from the work on the selected problem to the preferred problem, and it is useful for the worker and the client to discuss why the preferred problem was not selected. Was it possible to know this earlier in the work?
In cases where the worker and the client have completed the work in the agreed time it is unlikely that the selected problem proved to be the wrong one. As we saw in Chapter 5, difficulties in task completion often give early clues that the choice of problem is wrong.

3   *How much of the original goal do you think has been achieved?*
The client has been reminded of the goal during each session of work. In this final meeting, the worker asks the client to make a self-evaluation of progress towards the goal. From the time at which the written agreement was framed, the hope has been that the client would achieve the goal within the agreed period of time; if this is the case, then this provides a time for congratulation. The client's own part in this achievement should be stressed and reinforced.
It is the client's own view which is paramount. Usually the client's judgement will be the same as the worker's (at this stage in the work they will have developed the habit of sharing their perceptions). Occasionally, the worker may feel at odds with the client's evaluation; for example, clients who have been persistently hard on themselves when rating task completion may have been coaxed by the worker to recognize their strengths and to treat themselves a bit more generously. It is unusual for the client to give a wildly optimistic assessment of their achievement and in these circumstances a full discussion of Question 4 (below) becomes particularly important.
The worker may like to use a scale similar to that used in task review (Chapter 5), perhaps using numbers (5–4–3–2–1) or a verbal description (Completely/Mainly/Partly/Not Much/Not at all). The scale helps clients to quantify achievements, but its

purpose needs to be introduced carefully to avoid it smacking of the classroom.

AGREED REVIEW

CLIENT'S VIEW OF PROGRESS ON THE GOALS AND PROBLEMS

Is the selected problem the one you most wanted help with?
If not what is the problem which you would have liked help with?

How much of the original goal(s) has been achieved?
Note for each one how much progress was made e.g.
Completely/Mainly/Partly/Not much/Not at all?
If any of the goals were not reached why was this?

OTHER VIEWS OF PROGRESS

IS ANYTHING TO BE DONE NEXT?

Figure 6.1 An example of headings for a review session at the end of agreed work

4 *How much of the original goal do other people think you have achieved?*
In answering Question 3 clients have been talking about their subjective feelings at the end of the contact with the task-centred practitioner. These do not have to be questioned or justified. However, the balance between subjective feelings and objective assessments is a theme in task-centred practice, acknowledging the human need for confirmation from others. What other people say and do becomes part of the yardstick we use to judge our own behaviour.

When the written agreement was made, the worker emphasized the value of a clear and specific goal so that the client could measure the pace of progress towards achieving it. In addition, a clear goal was one which other people who were important to the client could understand. Clients may decide to ask these others (family or friends) what they think of their achievement. These opinions are neither more nor less important than the client's own evaluation – they merely provide another 'reading' to help clients make a sound assessment. The worker might ask clients if they want the worker's own opinion, too.

The actual or summarized views of other people important to the client are particularly useful when the worker feels the client's self-evaluation is idiosyncratic. Discussing how other people see the client's situation can help clients to make a balanced assessment.

5 *What do you think about this way of working?*
The strength of the task-centred method is the way it invites the client to understand the processes as well as the outcomes of the work. Whereas some techniques, such as paradoxical injunction, depend on the therapist's manipulation of the client's behaviour without the client's knowledge, techniques used in task-centred work, such as the goal gradient effect (see Chapter 5), depend on the client's proper understanding for their effectiveness.

Participation in the technicalities of the method is heightened when the client is asked to judge the task-centred way of working. This is not an assessment of the client's achievement or of the worker's skill but of the model of practice in itself.

The task-centred method of practice requires considerable professional skill, yet it is accessible to untrained people so that clients who have participated in task-centred sequences of work can describe what has happened and understand why it is effective. Perhaps this is a prerequisite for any system which claims to help with problems of living.

6 *How do you feel about coping in the future now that the Agreement has ended?*
The time limit which the worker and the client impose on their work is designed to avoid *drift* and to create *pressure*. Often regarded as a bad thing, pressure is a necessary component of change, though it has to be carefully managed. The reward is the achievement of something which the client wants to do.

The client has learnt about a particular way of problem-solving. If this has been a constructive experience, clients are ready to use the method themselves, as their own practitioner.

The worker should use the review to help the client move from the particular experience of this sequence of task-centred work to other potential areas for change. The sequence of learning is:

- Identify what has been happening in the particular circumstance (this sequence of task-centred work) and make sure the stages and processes are made explicit and understood.

- Generalize from this particular sequence in order to highlight the principles of task-centred work.

- Apply these principles to other specific problem areas in the client's life.

Most people who have completed the work are able to understand how they can apply the same process to other problems, though it is hard to keep up the pressure without somebody else's help. It is useful to have the resources of a friend or family member to do this (perhaps a person who has been involved in answering Question 4 above).

7 *Is any follow-up agreed? If yes, why?*
The benefit of a time limit is lost if there is slippage. For example, a student who knows that it is easy to get an extension on an essay deadline loses the pressure which helps to get the essay finished. However, there are occasions when work needs to continue beyond the time limit. Anticipated time extensions are:

- *Statutory obligations*
  The worker may have legal responsibilities which require further contact with the client. The task-centred sequence can be part of a longer involvement with the client, and a second Agreement may be negotiated for the next period. In this way lengthy involvements can be divided into manageable chunks of work.

- *A goal on the way to other goals*
  The client may have identified a small, achievable goal which puts them on the way to a long-term, more ambitious goal. For example, the ultimate goal of a person who has been resident in a hospital for most of her life may be to live independently in her own accommodation. She may want to

achieve smaller goals on the way, such as moving to a semi-independent hostel, and she and the worker might agree a series of task-centred sequences.

Unanticipated time extensions:

- *Nearly there*
  The judgement about how long it will take to achieve the goal may have been optimistic (though in our experience it is more likely to be achieved before time). Clearly, extra time should be agreed if success is imminent *and* the worker's continued involvement is needed to ensure this.

- *New and pressing problems emerge*
  Difficulties can emerge to overwhelm the original Agreement, which may have been re-negotiated to accommodate these new problems or frozen as crisis measures were taken (see Chapter 5). It is important to review the work, even if it has been chaotic and blown off course; is it possible to anticipate these difficulties in future and what can be learned from them? If conditions justify starting a fresh piece of task-centred work (as described in Chapter 2), a new Agreement can be negotiated.

Long-term contact and time-limited models

Some clients require continuing contact over long periods of time, because of long-term care or because of the statutory duties of the social services. There may be no difficulty in working in time-limited ways with these clients as the work may consist of a number of agreements running consecutively. For example, a child in care may receive a service based on a series of agreements with the ending of of each one providing a review point in the care programme. However, sometimes the pattern of work over these periods is one of shorter periods of active planning and longer periods of care or monitoring. An elderly person who has problems shopping and doing household tasks may work actively with a worker for a short period and then receive a service that is monitored periodically with a new agreement for active planning only considered if it is needed. In these cases it is worth making the distinction between *intervention* and *maintenance* (see Davies, 1981, on change and maintenance in social work).

Intervention can be considered as the period of the agreement, running through from problem to goal via tasks. Maintenance is the work undertaken on a regular basis to provide a consistent and relatively unchanged service. A period of intervention by a worker using task-centred methods might be followed by a period of maintenance in which, for example, a home help visits to provide home-based care. As long as the maintenance period continues there will be a need to review the situation at intervals, to see if circumstances have changed and if a new period of intervention is required. This pattern may also apply to supervision after a court appearance. A period of intervention may be followed by a period of maintenance when there is no active work, but there is a review of behaviour and problems to check on any specified elements of the supervision and to see if there is need for a repeated period of intervention.

Letting go

Task-centred practice is not a panacea for all the difficulties described at the beginning of this chapter. However, there are a number of ways in which these problems should be lessened.

- The end of the work is built into the beginning, so the final session does not come as a surprise. People have time to accommodate themselves to the worker's departure and view it as a positive milestone. Even so, it is important to acknowledge that ending is still the *only* area of task-centred work shown to be unpopular in the research (O'Connor and Reid, 1986).

- The client is left with *take-away skills* for problem-solving which can be used independently of the worker. The relationship between the client and the worker has been a means of acquiring these skills, not an end in itself, so the withdrawal of the worker does not leave a gap.

- The client knows more about what social work is and, hopefully, how the social work agency operates. This leads to a reduction in anxiety about access to social services and more clarity about what receiving a service means in practice. In these circumstances there is less need to cling on to a named person because there is more confidence about the nature and quality of future service if it is needed.

A client was comparing notes with her neighbour on a high-rise landing in the company of a student social worker. The client was discussing the task-centred work which the student had been using, and the neighbour – also a user of the social services – remarked, 'Why doesn't my social worker work like this?' In Chapter 1 we suggested that providing a popular service should be a consideration in choosing a practice model. We should also consider the harmful effects of timeless models of practice. These have been particularly well-documented in child care where drift has had seriously detrimental effects on the lives of children.

Building in endings from the very beginning helps to sharpen the focus of the work. Even when this ending is *artificial*, in the sense that continuing contact will be necessary, it provides a useful staging post for the partnership between client and worker.

Ending the work – case example

This follows the work described on pages 75–79.

The task-centred sequence of work with Mrs Northwich and Mrs Wall has ended, though the worker will continue to have a role in monitoring the situation as we described earlier in this chapter. We will take the goal detailed in Chapter 5 – *'I don't want to spend my evenings waiting in fear of Mrs Northwich banging on my door'* – to illustrate how the final evaluation of the task-centred work is undertaken.

1 *Is the Selected Problem the one which you most wanted help with?* The problem was stated as *'I get fearful and upset every evening waiting for Mrs Northwich to bang and shout at my front door'* and Mrs Wall felt that this (along with the problem in her relationship with her son) was the one she wanted most help with.

2 *If not, what is the problem which you would have liked help with?*
Mrs Wall continued to be troubled by Mrs Northwich's cats, but she felt that it was Mrs Northwich's behaviour that most upset her. She would still like to be able to change that behaviour and still wanted Mrs Northwich taken into a home, but recognized that these were not in her control.

3 *How much of the original goal do you think has been achieved?*
Mrs Wall felt that she was able to cope better. The situation with Mrs Northwich had improved a little, though not much, but she felt less fearful in the evenings and more in control of her own reactions. 'It feels more in proportion.'

4 *How much of the original goal do other people think you have achieved?*
The worker had suggested that Mrs Wall might talk to her son about their work together and ask him how much he felt she had achieved. Mrs Wall said this was a good idea, but didn't feel ready to do it yet.

5 *What do you think about this way of working?*
Mrs Wall said she thought it had helped her a lot. In particular she said she was glad that the worker 'hadn't given her all the

usual answers that everybody else had tried to fob me off with' when dealing with Mrs Northwich's behaviour; *get yourself out more, try to ignore it, stand up to her, etc.* She had felt listened to and had found the sessions very helpful.

6 *How do you feel about coping in the future now that the Agreement has ended?*
Mrs Wall had made another arrangement with the volunteer organizer to go to the library. The organizer had suggested a luncheon club, but Mrs Wall didn't want to pursue that idea – *'I'm not very sociable.'* She wanted to be able to phone the worker if she wanted help again.

7 *Is any follow-up agreed? If yes, why?*
No follow-up was agreed with Mrs Wall, but the worker explained that contact would continue with Mrs Northwich to monitor her situation, which might get worse. No pattern had emerged which could explain why Mrs Northwich had quiet weeks and why she had noisy weeks. Mrs Wall was still upset by this, but felt more equipped to cope with it.

The profile of task-centred work

If the 'shape' of task-centred practice could be presented graphically it would be short and fat. It is a relatively intense burst of work in a brief period of time. Practitioners need to ask whether the shape of their agency's workload will accommodate these kinds of intervention (Hari, 1977). An agency whose work patterns are typically long and thin – diffused contacts over extended periods of time – might find it difficult to support task-centred interventions. We have seen that it is possible to have a series of short, fat interventions with the same client when long-term involvement is required.

The time taken in a short, fat intervention (say, an hour a week for eight weeks) can be the same as the time taken over long, thin ones (say, an hour a month over eight months) – both equal eight hours. However, the change from diffuse to intense patterns of work requires 'lift' in the form of support from the agency. The most difficult aspect for a worker wishing to practise a new method is *starting out*, and a sound assessment of the profile of the agency's workload will be useful in judging the size of the effort needed to move into task-centred gear.

7 Pointers for Practice

In this chapter we look at some of the misconceptions about task-centred practice and relate these to a better understanding of the scope of task-centred work. We review what the research suggests clients value and how task-centred practice measures up to this. In conclusion, we summarize the essential aspects of the task-centred model.

Misconceptions

The name *task-centred* practice rightly identifies the centrality of tasks but can lead to a one-dimensional image of this way of working. Misunderstandings about the scope of task-centred work also arise as a result of the success in establishing itself as a distinctive model of work, perhaps suggesting it is there to be dusted off for use in particular circumstances with specific clients.

Is task-centred social work a specialist method which certain practitioners can use in some appropriate cases, or is it an approach to practice which can inform all encounters between clients and workers? A discussion of the following eight typical responses to task-centred social work will help us to answer this question.

1 'It's only about practical things'
Task-centred pieces of work often reduce to ordinary, even mundane aspects of life. One practitioner who regularly worked with

parents and adolescents in conflict noticed a recurring pattern of tasks around household chores, especially washing up, to the extent that she thought of naming it *pots and pans social work*. We all have a hankering for bright-lights social work, cracking long-held family secrets à la Pincus and Dare (1978), yet it is the everyday behaviours which are most accessible to change and the ones which people often feel are the most important.

There are parallels in health, where improvements over the last hundred years owe more to the unglamorous work of public health officials and sewage workers than to hi-tec surgery or those rare *Eureka!* moments in the medical laboratory.

Strip away the veneer and the social work office can show all the machismo of a building site, with emergency protection orders and emergency admissions notched on professional belts. If current dramas are short in supply, it is always possible to find substitutes by unearthing emotional crises from a client's past. *Pots and pans social work* can appear tame by comparison, so task-centred practitioners need to be able to explain their work carefully to colleagues and managers.

Pots and pans social work can have spin-offs. Mrs Green and her 13 year old son, Michael, were at the point of breakdown when the social worker helped them to negotiate a written agreement about chores in the house, following suggestions from them about the use of a rota. The task-centred work finished successfully, with Mrs Green and Michael agreeing that they had largely achieved their goal of arguing less. (A rather fuzzy goal in this instance, but they knew what they meant, and a daughter not directly involved in the work confirmed their success.) Two months later, Michael chanced by the social worker in the street. He told the worker how he had been talking a lot more with his mother, who had since revealed that the man whom he saw infrequently and had always understood to be his father wasn't, and that another distantly-known man was. Michael was pleased rather than angry that his mother had found the courage to tell him this. He wanted to meet his father, but first he wanted to prepare himself by using the social worker to rehearse what he might say.

That makes rather more interesting reading than describing how Michael and Mrs Green negotiated their agreement about the pots and pans – and perhaps it also feels more *professional*. Yet the most difficult piece of work had been the negotiations over the domestic chores, and these had been instrumental in opening the channels of communication between mother and son.

2 'It doesn't get to the root of the problems'

Tina Jones wants some money . . . She wants some money to buy shoes for the children . . . She doesn't have the money because she spent the last of her giro paying back her friend . . . She borrowed money from her friend to take out a rental on a video-recorder . . . She rented the video-recorder to keep the children entertained . . . She cannot entertain the children by taking them out because her giro cheque is too small . . . Her giro cheque is too small because government policy towards the poor is neglectful . . . Government policy is neglectful because of its philosophy of self-help . . . This policy has popular support because the government keeps getting re-elected . . . The government gets re-elected because the voting system splinters opposition votes . . . The voting system . . . etc.

What do we mean by 'getting to the root of the problems'? If this means following causal connections to their roots, we can see that, *reductio ad absurdum* the duty social worker faced with Tina Jones's request for money must first change the parliamentary voting system in Great Britain. There are other difficulties in chasing causal connections to reach the suppose roots of problems, not least that the chain might be flawed, that it can easily become circular and that the client and worker might follow different causal chains.

It is more significant to consider the meanings which clients attribute to an event and the line of reasoning which they use to explain it. Equally important is the decision which the client and worker need to take about where to stop the line of reasoning, where to settle at a point for action. Assuming a mandate for the work (see Chapter 2), three principles should help to decide where that point is:

- *The client's line of reasoning*
  Wherever possible, it is the client's own line of reasoning which is followed. This may be prompted by the worker via the kinds of question being asked, but clients must be encouraged to follow their own reasoning and offer their own meanings. For example, a client who sees religious meanings in events is more likely to understand why and how change is possible if this is defined in spiritual terms, no matter how alien this feels to a

secular worker. If following the client's line of reasoning proves impossible, there may be no agreement for further work.

• *The point of action is within the client's influence*
The line of reasoning might be long, as in the example of Tina Jones, and it may differ from the worker's, but the point of action should be 'near enough' to the client to be amenable to change. So, the system of parliamentary voting would not be a good point at which to settle for action!

• *The point of action is negotiated with the client*
The decision about where to intervene in the line of reasoning should be discussed with the client and seen as relevant.

Helping people to become aware of how they reason is an essential aspect of task-centred work and can help the client to practise more effective ways of explaining what is happening. This, in itself, can feel like an increase in control.

'Getting to the root of problems' can also indicate a desire to ferret into the client's emotional past. The three principles outlined above should apply in these circumstances; if the client's reasoning takes a backward path, follow it as far as the client chooses and as far as it is practicable to take action. Practised properly, task-centred work enables clients to dig deep into their problems, but only *if they want to*. Current problems may have long histories, but it is a fallacy to suppose that change is necessarily dependent on a knowledge of the history. Indeed, there are brief therapies which start with the goal and leave the problems untouched (de Shazer, 1985). After all, it is possible to start untangling a ball of wool and to learn how to keep it untangled without knowing how it got tangled in the first place.

The case of Mrs Green and Michael described earlier in this chapter illustrates two crucial points in this respect. The first is the fallacy which suggests that present problems are necessarily 'caused by' past histories, that the family arguments were the direct result of Mrs Green's secret. Such determinism is simplistic and fails to allow for the fact that although A may have caused B to start to happen x years ago, B may now be happening independently of A. It is more helpful to think in terms of the client's line of reasoning than causal connections.

Secondly, even if a causal link is made, working on the historical cause of the problem is not the only way of solving it. Clearly, the opposite happened with Mrs Green and Michael; they were able to confront and resolve 'young' problems without an understanding of 'old' ones. It was only after they resolved young problems that they wanted to discuss old ones.

It is important to emphasize that the worker did not undertake the task-centred work as a way of getting to older problems. Mrs Green, Michael and the worker were sincere in wanting to work with the younger problems, and this was essential to their success. Mrs Green decided she could handle the older problems on her own, building on her experience of task-centred work.

3 'We do it already'
The absence of any selected problem, agreed goal or time limit, let alone any shared record of the work, does not always shake a worker's conviction that he or she is practising task-centred work. Too often, task-centred practice is loosely associated with a certain mood or style of practice – brisk and practical. At worst it means telling the client what to do.

The reality is in striking contrast to the image. Far from brisk, the task-centred practitioner's main quality is a painstaking, thorough approach. Task-centred work is practical, in the sense that it is active and focuses on what is achievable, but it is theoretical in two senses of the word; it is carefully founded on theories of practice (see Chapter 1) and it harnesses the worker's and the client's powers of reasoning. To this extent it is a course in applied philosophy. Equating task-centred work with telling people what to do is parody. The clarion call of task-centred practice is *partnership* and the success of the method rests on the discovery of what the client wants, how this fits with what the worker and client can and should do and the negotiations which take place around this.

It would be wrong to be precious about task-centred practice and to define it in a tight fashion; clearly, the styles of individual workers and the responses of different clients will fashion a unique example of task-centred work each time it is practised. However, it is important to get a thorough grasp of the mechanics of the model, its working parts and the way they operate in practice, before experimenting with customized models. When we feel confident with the details of practice we can cut corners successfully and modify the structure of the model to meet different circumstances.

Real changes in practice should feel different, even strange. These feelings are not to be distrusted, but welcomed as an indication that new ground is being broken and that the method is taking hold. It is a step towards competence, when innovations in style and method can be built on a sound foundation.

4 'At least it's easy to learn how to do task-centred work'

An example of professional snobbery was reported by a student social worker who, having rehearsed task-centred practice in workshops at college, wished to use it with one of his clients (Doel, 1989). His practice teacher was not sympathetic and complained that 'they only teach task-centred at college because it's easy to teach'. It would be convenient if this were true (Marsh, 1990).

There are three ways in which the 'simpleness' of task-centred practice is deceptive. The first relates to the values which support this method of work. Who can disagree with the need for honesty, openness, clarity and partnership? Yet these are qualities which it is very difficult to achieve, both professionally and personally. In particular, social workers have often learnt to equate professional skill with the ability to interpret what lies behind actions and words, and not necessarily the ability to share these interpretations with the users of the services. Our experiences training many practitioners to use task-centred work is that the professional jargon associated with diagnostic approaches is a great hindrance and that the necessary *unlearning* is very difficult.

A second difficulty is to be found in the need to balance systematic with responsive communicataions in the direct work with clients. Task-centred work is often equated with being systematic. However, the responsive element in task-centred work is also crucial. It is not an easy skill to balance the need for structure and system in an intervention with the need for empathic responsiveness to the client's immediate concerns (see Reid and Epstein, 1972, Chapter 6).

Finally, task-centred practice requires creativity to be successful. The systems approach relies on wide-thinking to prove new insights and fresh initiatives. It takes creative energy to move away from tired thinking and to use the task-centred framework in a flexible way.

Task-centred practice is a relatively easy method to understand and a relatively easy method to communicate to others but, unfortunately, it is not an easy method to learn how to practise.

5 'It doesn't address anti-oppressive practice'

Social workers work with people who are at the margins of society. Many of these people feel oppressed by their relative powerlessness to influence this position. One of the most important aspects of the social worker's job is to work in anti-oppressive ways, always seeking to increase the power of people who are discriminated against in a society which is based on white, male power.

Task-centred practice might be criticized for focusing on the individual case (if not always the individual person) and thus locating the *problem* with the individual. An uncritical view of the social influences on an individual's circumstances would lead to blinkered vision, and unrealistic expectations about the ability of individuals to change things. However, in a modest way, task-centred work does contribute to anti-oppressive practice by helping people to understand the context of their problems and by giving them the know-how to achieve small changes. It is one of a whole series of methods (which include the bullet and the ballot box) by which changes can be made.

The largest contribution which task-centred practice can make to anti-oppressive practice stems from its openness to the client's definition of the world. The task-centred worker does not seek to interpret the client's framework to fit another, nor to patronize clients by assuming that they are as all-powerless as the oppressors are assumed to be all-powerful.

Is the task-centred method in itself a white, male, middle-class way of thinking and doing? In other words, are problem-solving approaches *per se* associated with the dominant groups in society, and the task-centred practitioner merely an agent to teach some of the bystanders how to play the game? The research suggests that there is both truth and myth in this view. Task-centred practice is not restricted to particular groups in society; it has been used successfully and well-received by all groups (black and white, male and female, young and old; see Appendix 2 for a full task-centred bibliography). However, part of the reason for its good reception might be the fact that it does help marginalized individuals to participate in society's games.

We think that the case example which followed Chapters 2 to 6 illustrates anti-oppressive practice. The work increased the power of individuals who are often left out of decision-making (the elderly). The worker in this case might also have views on the role of women as carers in the community (all the actors in this example are female) and might seek to introduce these views into the work. In some circumstances sharing ideas about anti-oppressive practice can be very liberating and at other times it can be patronizing. Workers must take cues from clients to know how far they should introduce their own frames of reference.

6 'It's only useful in certain cases'

Practitioners often talk of using certain methods of practice 'when appropriate'. How is 'appropriate' defined in task-centred work? The image of appropriateness in task-centred work is of practical, short-term problems with reasonable, articulate clients. Nothing too heavy and not too much conflict. We hope that this book has helped to dispel that image of task-centred work, but wish to point to those areas of practice which seem to be most amenable to the task-centred approach.

- *Administration*
  The gatekeeping functions of welfare bureaucracies occupy more social work time than many would want. Telephone applications, bus passes and car badges are important to the applicants, but they do not require the panoply of a written agreement, a sledge hammer to crack a nut. They rely on fair procedures, clear criteria and a minimum of discretionary power; as such they require *administrative* rather than social work skills.

- *Urgency*
  When a crisis arises it is necessary to take quick, prompt action. Although task-centred principles might inform the work during the crisis, there are likely to be over-riding principles concerned with safety and immediacy. Task-centred work might take place subsequent to the crisis, but the painstaking approach of the problem exploration and the longer vision of the written agreement are not called for during the crisis. The skills of the *accident and emergency services* are more appropriate than social work skills.

- *Policing*
  In those circumstances when no working agreement is possible and the work consists of surveillance, investigation and possible prosecution, it is evident that task-centred work is inappropriate. This work requires the skills of *policing*.

Social workers are called upon to work in the three areas above but this is not necessarily 'social work'. It is right and proper that the social work perspective should be included in these three functions, but it is the respective skills of administration, accident/ emergency and policing which are paramount in these areas.

Figure 7.1 The territory of social work

The ground which lies between these three poles is large and is wholly amenable to task-centred work. All of this area of practice, social work's heartland, is open to task-centred practice (and we should acknowledge that social workers and police are, for example, to be found working in each other's heartlands). Task-centred work is not a method of practice peculiar to a select group of clients – it can be used in all circumstances where social work is practised.

The ability to reason

The major factor determining the success, rather than the appropriateness of task-centred work, is the client's ability to reason (and the social worker's, for that matter). In those cases where social work is appropriate (Figure 7.1) but where reasoning is seriously impaired, such as some forms of mental illness, people with considerable learning difficulties or a great degree of confusion, task-centred work is often not possible in direct work with that person.

The case example which we have used to illustrate the various stages of the model has shown that it is possible to use the task-centred approach *around* the person, as a means to help others to help.

7 'My agency's procedures will conflict with this model'

There is no doubt that there will be occasions when an agency's procedures seem to be in conflict with a task-centred model of practice. However, this is not something which is particular to this one approach. There is an almost inevitable tension between some of the demands of practice and some of the organizational procedures that an agency wants its staff to follow. It would be unusual for any individual worker to be able to follow procedures to the last letter in all of their work; procedures simply cannot be so comprehensive in a professional agency. This should not be interpreted as a plea to go against agency guidelines, nor a suggestion that they are unnecessary; it is simply acknowledging the fact that procedures are not all-encompassing and it is vital that they are interpreted in a professional way. The rationale for not following procedures is the more interesting issue, rather than the conflict between procedures and what is actually done.

In what circumstances (apart from incompetence) do procedures and practice differ? First, workers may feel that a short cut or change would be easier in certain circumstances and that the short cut would still be in the spirit of the procedures. Secondly, workers may think that a procedure applied in a particular case goes against the best interests of a client. These two questions could be seen as ones of *professional interpretation* and *professional challenge*.

The detail of these two areas merits more coverage than we can give it here; the issue that concerns us is the manner in which task-centred practice is likely to affect these two issues. In connection with *professional interpretation* the practitioner needs to reflect on the underlying principles of procedures and of their own practice, and make a judgement about the degree of conflict or similarity between the two. Task-centred practice is unlikely to sharpen the ability to judge, but a good task-centred practitioner should certainly be alert to the underlying principles of actions (as we have seen, the mandate for actions is a crucial issue in task-centred work). The model highlights the rationale for actions and being aware of this rationale is useful for *professional interpretation*. It is also useful for *professional challenge*. When a worker thinks that procedures should be challenged, the clarity about input and out-come in task-centred work may be very important to the client.

Agency procedures will conflict with professional judgements at times. Task-centred work does not exacerbate this difficulty and it could provide a rather better basis for juding the merit of such conflict.

8 'You can't use this model to investigate child abuse'

It is vital that child abuse investigation and intervention should be carried out to the highest possible standard. The importance of this work, the risk attached to wrong decisions and the emotional issues involved, all lead to a great deal of sensitivity about the relevance of any practice innovation to child protection work. Task-centred practice stresses the need for clear and explicit statements of the reasons for intervention and this is seen by some workers as a block to the investigative procedures needed in child protection. The essence of the argument is that putting cards on the table, as encouraged by the model, may lead to clients being unwilling to reveal important information.

Two main points need to be addressed in considering this issue. First, how much can intentions be successfully hidden from the clients? Secondly, how likely is it that recognition of the worker's investigative task will lead to rejection of contact? It is probably much more difficult than we think to disguise the real intentions lying behind any questions which attempt a covert assessment of the possibility of child abuse. If the questions are addressed to an abuser, or to someone who knows about the abuse, that individual is likely to be sensitive to the possibility of investigation. Hints and nuances that we can't disguise may well lead to the person guessing the real intent at an early stage. Also, the ability to ask highly pertinent questions will be limited if these questions need to be wrapped up to make them look innocent. So the scope for covert investigation by questioning the suspected abuser, or someone who knows of the abuse, is restricted. It is unlikely that sound pro-fessional judgement will lead to this kind of approach, and the emphasis on an above-board approach in task-centred practice should be perfectly acceptable. It is possible to engage in covert investigation where the issue of disguising one's intentions does not arise. The telephone call to the doctor, as a result of suspicions about a client, may be undertaken without informing the person being investigated. Is this compatible with task-centred practice?

These difficulties are not peculiar to task-centred practice. Covert investigation with third parties may be necessary, and in these circumstances a worker will eventually have to face up to informing the client of the concerns and of the covert practice that has taken place. This is likely to provide a bad basis for future work, but such an investigation may be the only way a worker believes it is possible to proceed to make sure that the child is not pressured into silence by the suspected abuser before there is an opportunity to disclose. Task-centred practitioners are in the same position as others on this issue.

What clients value

How should we evaluate task-centred practice? Who is in the best position to judge whether it is successful in what it sets out to achieve, and how do we know that these ends are, in themselves, worth achieving?

Each separate piece of task-centred practice can be evaluated 'locally' by the client and the worker and by others who are not parties to the work but able to comment on its effects. In addition, we can look outside the arena of task-centred work to broader-based client studies in order to see what these tell us about what clients value. The task-centred model can then be set alongside those aggregate findings.

Finding out what clients find attractive is an important though not unique measure. If we look at other services which affect our lives (for example, dentistry, school education, British Gas) we can see how a survey of what patients, pupils, parents and customers valued would give us important, though not exclusive, clues about good practices. Let us take some of the areas which Sainsbury (1989) identified when reviewing client opinion studies in Britain since 1970. This provides the beginnings of a yardstick to measure task-centred work.

Clients value understanding the intentions and purposes of the worker

Clients wish to *understand* the purposes of the worker even if they are not in agreement with them. In task-centred practice the 'getting to yes' process (Fisher and Ury, 1982) is emphasized as an important factor, but there are occasions when work must go ahead on the basis of *acceptance*, what we might call 'getting to OK'. In these circumstances, clients want to know the basis of any disagreement and the task-centred model requires this to be explicit.

Clients value contributing to the work of the service

In general, social work has not got to grips with the potential of reciprocal relationships. It is neater and less risky to see people in a one-dimensional fashion, as recipients or donors, but never both at the same time. This view is reinforced by bureaucratic rules of conduct in public service and professional codes of practice.

The task-centred model addresses the issue of the client's contribution to the service indirectly, by stressing the client's own role in achieving success and by discussing how the worker's experience of using the method with the client will influence future practice (see Chapter 6). People who have used task-centred methods usually feel some sense of success, no matter how modest, and are aware of their contribution to it.

Clients value receiving help speedily

Fire-fighters do not wait to see if fires will burn themselves out, or hope that a downpour will come along to quash the flames, yet this is the kind of strategy which is sometimes adopted for social work. Some citizens are required to jump through many hoops before they can become a client, whilst others become clients all too quickly and unwillingly. It is a strange situation.

A speedy response to the initial request for help is crucial to effective task-centred work. Speed is affected by staffing levels, priorities and the rate of work coming in; it is also determined by the way in which that work is managed and practised.

How do teams break into virtuous or vicious circles of work? Increased staffing and improvements in other community services are obvious factors, but perhaps the prevailing model of practice is also important? It is clear that the short, fat interventions which characterize task-centred work require control over time and that they will also clear work more quickly, but instituting these changes in agencies with long-term profiles may be difficult (Hari, 1977).

Clients value the worker's ability to respond to feelings not always expressed

In social work practice a balance is necessary between two extremes. On the one hand is a kind of practice which is highly interpretive, looking for meanings which it is not possible to challenge or corroborate and working to an agenda which is more buried than hidden. On the other hand is a practice which is highly rational, dependent on the command of language and logic and blind to symbolic meanings and irrational forces. Task-centred practice must beware the latter extreme.

The skilled practitioner is one who is able to take soundings which enable the work to go at the right pace for the client. A model of practice which is designed to help people gain more control over their lives by using problem-solving techniques must rely on the development of reason; however, there are many different ways of doing this. Taking a different kind of example, persons wishing to increase control over their lives by improving physical fitness, would at some point need to exercise the body's muscles. However, first they may need emotional support to get to that point, and intellectual work to decide on what strategy best achieves the aim. They would not have relied solely on physical means to achieve greater physical fitness. It is a mistake to assume that the methods used to achieve a goal have to be congruent with the goal itself.

Returning to task-centred practice, it is not necessary to be 'emotional' to work on emotions and feelings. The task-centred practitioner should pick up non-verbal communications and acknowledge irrational feelings and experiences. Since reasoning is not subject to any natural law, but is a highly subjective affair, workers need to be able to understand the client's system of belief. This means avoiding the interpretation of it to make it fit the worker's own system.

Clients value the worker's concern even if change is not possible

Most people are able to distinguish between qualities in the practitioner and the outcome of the work. This is not to suggest that the outcome of work is unimportant, but to emphasize the importance which people attach to the way they are treated during the work. Fisher et al. (1986) found that the parents of children coming in and out of care could make separate judgements about what happened and how it happened; so they could be unhappy that their child was taken into care but make positive statements about the worker's behaviour (and vice versa).

It is helpful to know that clients value the journey as well as the arrival. Task-centred practice focuses on outcomes, but this does not mean that processes are neglected. Clients are carefully involved in the processes of problem-solving, but these are more keenly understood if they are related to a specific outcome. We should remember that process which looks effortless is not necessarily process which is overlooked.

Clients value the worker's ability to exercise care even when exercising control

Sainsbury (1989) discusses the balance between needs and risks in social work practice and the trend over the last decade has been towards practice governed by procedures to minimize risk. It is proper to urge a more careful calculation of risk in the wake of numerous well-publicized examples of failure to protect children. However, it is no surprise to note that people value workers who can appreciate their own difficulties alongside the need to protect others.

The mandate for involvement described in Chapter 2 gives a framework for task-centred practitioners to determine when there are two clients whose interests may be both separate and inter-twined (for example, a severely depressed mother and her child at risk). This helps the worker to keep the two sets of needs in mind and to consider the kinds of work agreements necessary to reflect these needs and risks. The protection of the child may be the priority but this does not entail an abandonment of the mother's suffering.

Seven key points

The following seven points are key areas for task-centred prac-titioners to bear in mind at all stages of their practice.

1 The basis for intervention
It is important to be as clear as possible about the mandate for intervention, since the client's agreement or the clear mandate of

a court order should be the exclusive basis of intervention. All active intervention with a client should be on the basis of a clear statement of a problem or problems; the statement should specify whether the problems are openly agreed by clients or mandated by a court.

There will be a time when the status of the contact is not yet clear, when initial discussions are taking place or investigations are in progress. This stage should be as short as possible and will often end in no further action. There will also be grey areas such as child protection conferences; the legitimacy of these in the eyes of the client may be the key factor in deciding how far they provide a mandate based on the client's agreement.

2   Small, visible successes, not large, hidden failures

Of the action techniques used in task-centred practice, the ability to be specific and to help others to be specific is one of the most important. This applies to the description and analysis of problems, the definition of goals, and the development of tasks. It also refers to the worker's ability to describe the processes of the work with the client. The worker and the client should aim for a small, achievable success in a particular part of the client's life.

This is a departure from the grand reformism of social work in bygone days. The desire for radical change, at either a personal or a societal level, is understandable, but leads to disappointment. People can achieve modest increases in control of their lives and even the slowing down of an inevitable deterioration can induce a feeling of success.

Goals should be within the client's capacity to achieve and there should be agreed, observable criteria so that the client and the worker (and perhaps other interested parties) can assess whether a goal has been achieved. Before embarking on the work, the client and the worker should be able to answer the question, *how will we know when we have been successful?*

In situations where individuals are agreeing goals for others (for example, for young children), the others should be involved in agreeing those goals as far as is appropriate to their age. When practitioners allow adults to negotiate on behalf of children, they should check that the child is being involved up to the limits of what is possible.

3 The central position of tasks

Tasks are the central working tool in the intervention. After a written agreement has been made, an integral part of any interview will be the negotiation of new tasks and the review of tasks which have been completed. Each task is reviewed and, in constructing tasks, alternatives are considered. It is important to identify what kind of task it is – a session task, a practitioner task or a client task, so that it is clear who will be doing it and when.

Workers should not become dependent upon one kind of task, but should use a variety of session, practitioner and client tasks. The relationship of individual tasks to the achievement of the goal should be emphasized, and the worker should ensure that the client is properly prepared to undertake any tasks.

The word *task* conjures a very practical activity, but it is important to remember the value of psychological or mental tasks, especially in work with inactive or immobilized people.

4 Measuring progress within a time limit

Task-centred practice is an open way of working which encourages the worker and the client to share their views and beliefs about the situation, giving regular feedback to each other. This openness is systematic, with the worker asking clients to make their own assessment of progress towards the goals. Progress is seen as an incremental process, with failed tasks viewed positively as learning opportunities. Most of all, progress is measured against an agreed endpoint at a *specific time*, so the time limit acts as a motivator.

Active intervention should be brief rather than lengthy, with agreed time limits for both the overall agreement and for individual tasks. Longer-term work may take place as a series of short-term agreements, each of which should be as short as practically possible, ideally not exceeding three months.

5 Learning from experience

The work with the particular client should be generalized in two ways. First, for the client's own purposes the problem-solving process should be reviewed to see how the client can use the same methods with other current problems or future anticipated ones. Secondly, the experience of this particular sequence of work should be available (in a form which preserves the client's anonymity) to other practitioners, adding to the body of research about *what works*, when and with whom in social work practice.

A practice model like task-centred practice can give practitioners a common language to discuss their work in an effort to refine the wheel rather than re-invent it. Task-centred practitioners should be research-minded. In Britain and the United States there is an increasing body of research specific to task-centred practice.

6 The skills of task-centred practice

The most delicate balance to achieve in task-centred work is that between the need for communications with the client which are systematic and communications which are responsive. Writing in 1972, Reid and Epstein defined systematic communication as 'responses which can logically be expected to further completion of the step being worked on'. Communication is responsive to the extent that it: '1) expresses interest in the client's communications and recognition of their value; 2) conveys empathic understanding, that is, comprehension and appreciation of the central meanings of the client's verbal and nonverbal messages; 3) builds upon the client's own communications' (p. 127).

Judging when to follow a client down a conversational cul-de-sac is not easy, because it is often too late when we realize it leads nowhere. How can tangential issues brought up by the client be related to the central themes already identified? Skilled practitioners are aware of the patterns in their communications with other people; they can compensate for a tendency either to focus excessively, or to follow every lead given by the client.

7 The scope of task-centred practice

We asked earlier in this chapter whether task-centred practice is a specialist method of practice or whether it is a general approach to social work which can inform all encounters between workers and clients. By looking at some of the misconceptions we hoped to highlight what task-centred practice is, by looking at what it is not.

The task-centred model prescribes a set of sequences of work, detailed and illustrated in Chapters 3 to 6. At this *pure* level, task-centred social work is a very specific method of working, one which practitioners may feel is relevant to some but not all of their work with clients. It is a method with a specific technology, requiring a specific training.

However, the principles which underpin task-centred practice constitute something more than a particular method of working. The concern to develop a partnership between the worker and the client, a partnership founded on openness and agreement, is something which should be a part of all our dealings with users of the social services. The framework which helps us to decide whether and how we can work with somebody, the mandate for intervention, is applicable in all circumstances.

The search for a partnership might take a long time, might falter and might eventually prove impossible, but the steps taken in that search can be true to the spirit of task-centred work.

A Note for the American Reader

From its early development in the Reid and Shyne study, *Brief and Extended Casework* (1969), task-centered practice has had strong American roots. Indeed, a British text advocating task-centered social work to the American reader may seem like 'carrying coals to Newcastle' and there may appear to be no need for this *Note* – the new outline and the new developments contained in this text should be able to stand on their own. To a large degree they can, nevertheless American readers will want an explanation of the British context in order to make best use of the material in this book. They may also be curious about the history of task-centered practice in the United Kingdom.

Both authors are familiar with the American context. At the time of writing this *Note*, Mark Doel was working in the Regional Research Institute at the Graduate School of Social Work in Portland, Oregon, having also spent a year as a social worker in Philadelphia; and Peter Marsh has many American links through the *Social Work in Partnership* research program.

The context of social work practice in Britain

Central government provides the legislative framework which entitles citizens to consideration for social services from their local government (local authority). Perhaps the most striking characteristic of the British social work scene was the dominance of the public

110

services, with relatively small private and non-profit (voluntary) sectors. Most students who train as social workers in the United Kingdom still expect to find employment in public agencies, largely in Social Services Departments and Probation Services in England and Wales or Social Work Departments in Scotland. The Social Services Department is a local government agency which, since 1971, has housed all kinds of social work, from cradle to grave. In the case example used at the end of chapters two to six, it is likely that the social worker, the day center worker and the home warden would all be employed by the Social Services Department.

Another striking contrast with the American system is the financing of British services and the relatively small impact that this has on the direct contacts between practitioners and clients. There may be a financial assessment to see whether the citizen is liable to pay for a service such as home care, but most direct services from social workers are freely available. The extent of payment for services such as residential care is usually related to a formula based on a person's income and expenditure. In general, social workers do not supplement a client's income directly and the primary duty of income maintenance falls on the social security system, funded by central government.

In the case example in this book, it is likely that Mrs Northwich would pay little or nothing for the home warden and day center services, and neither she nor Mrs Wall would pay for the social worker's services. However, the availability of home care and day care services varies considerably from one local authority to another.

Private social work practice has increased dramatically in the United States since the early 1980s, with diminished resources for public services and an emphasis on private sector participation through contracting. The laws of vendorship passed by legislatures in over half of the states allows social workers with appropriate credentials to bill insurance companies for third party payments, and this has also had an impact on the growth of private practice.

In Britain, private practice remains rare. In terms of social work, private insurance is insignificant, though private *health* insurance has grown with encouragement from Conservative Governments in power since 1979, and private contracting in the public services has also increased considerably. The British scene is generally more politicized than the American one and private practice would be interpreted by many as a failure to support the public system.

There have been far-reaching legislative changes in Britain

recently in both community care and children's services. In addition, the organization of services has been undergoing large changes in many of the social services departments (the most common being a reorganization away from generalist and towards specialist practice). Set this in the context of controversial changes in the way in which local government is funded and a new framework for the education and training of social workers, and the American reader will be able to understand the dizzy conditions for human service professionals in Britain in the 1990s.

Task-centered practice in Britain

The Reid and Shyne study found interested audiences in Britain, and it was common to find Reid and Epstein's *Task-Centered Casework* on the reading lists of social work training courses after its publication in 1972. No doubt many of these courses offered more than a passing reference to the task-centered model, especially when systems theory moved center stage. However, it is difficult to say how much of the 'technology' of the model was known or made available, and the first systematic training programs were probably those developed in the late 1970s at the National Institute of Social Work in London. During the 1980s, the task-centered model put down more research and training roots in the United Kingdom.

It is not easy to judge how widely the task-centered method is used. Despite the adverse climate for public services in Britain during the 1980s, there were developments favoring methods such as task-centered practice, making it well-placed for the current decade. A growing consumer-oriented movement has made progress in penetrating the service industries and encouraging them to be more responsive. British consumers are not yet as robust as their American counterparts, but they are learning to confront a culture of paternalism.

Paternalism in the *professions* has also been challenged during the past decade. The British public's consistent support for a public health service has not diminished criticism of the secrecy and obfuscation which often surrounds medical practices. In the social services, the rhetoric of user power may be stronger than the reality, but there have been definite gains and, at the very least, agencies cannot be seen to be neglecting the user's voice. The social workers' professional association, the British Association of Social Workers, has long advocated for clients to have access to their case records.

The values underpinning task-centered practice are more than sympathetic to this customer-oriented movement; a focus on partnership rather than diagnosis, and on strengths rather than deficits emphasizes clients as fellow citizens, with the right to expect responsive services. The evidence on both sides of the Atlantic is that task-centered social work is well-received and that it can be an attractive model for agencies wanting to have a clearer idea about what kinds of service goals are achievable and an understanding of the outcomes of its work.

On the other hand, the misconceptions surrounding task-centered work are considerable. We think that the careful responses to the model's detractors (presented in chapter seven) are as relevant in the United States as in the United Kingdom.

Customized for the British audience

American readers who are already familiar with the task-centered model will notice many modifications to the task-centered lexicon used in this book. These changes have been necessary because of the different tolerances of British and American practitioners and clients. Feedback from clients has been especially useful in making these changes, based on the principle of 'plain English' wherever possible.

For example, because it is not obvious to a British ear what a 'target problem' is, we describe it as a 'selected problem.' In speech we would be more likely to say 'the problem I chose,' but most people accept that the written word is more formal than the spoken one. The *Newspaper method* described in this book is helping us to make the task-centered language more user-friendly and is proving to be an effective way of helping individuals and groups to make priorities in a creative fashion. It is a method which has a broad application; we have used it in one to one problem-solving, in small training groups and at large conferences as an entertaining way to focus feedback from work groups to plenary sessions.

'Task' is not an alluring word in Britain, and for this reason we replaced it with 'work' for a while in our training and practice. It has to be admitted that *task-centered social work* is not the greatest name tag. However, as we explain in chapter five, the concept of 'task' is central to the model, and we have no better alternative to offer, so 'task' it remains.

The differences between the ways in which the Americans and the British use the same words are subtle and pervasive, and go well beyond the differences in spelling words like *task-cent(e)red practice*. For example, there are parallel controversies in both countries over the ways in which concepts are described. In the United States there is the move from the term *minorities* to *people of color* and to the notion of *culturally competent practice*. In Britain there are moves from *anti-discriminatory* to *anti-oppressive* practice.

If the changes in the use of these words signify a more sophisticated attempt to discuss the issues and ideas which lie behind them, then they are to be welcomed. The term *physically challenged*, for example, says something very different from *physically disabled* or *physically handicapped*. If, however, these changes serve only to alienate me from you because I consider my language to be more correct than yours, then the effect is highly corrosive.

We ask both the American reader and the British reader to look for the meaning behind our words; whether there is agreement or disagreement, let it be with our meanings and not with our words.

Mark Doel, Portland, Oregon
Peter Marsh, Sheffield, England
May, 1991

Appendix 1   Checklists

Chapter 2 – The mandate for Work

Is the purpose of the intervention clear?
'There are four ways in which purpose may be "knotted" in such a way as to defeat initial efforts to define the client:

- Clarity of the request for help
- Acknowledgement of the problems
- Problems involving other people
- Ability of the agency to respond.' (pages 13–14)

How far can the client understand this model of practice?
'Central to the task-centred practice is the belief that the client's own understanding of the model increases its effectiveness, so that practitioners need to be able to describe the process of the work as well as the outcome. It is not, therefore, a tool to be used on a client, but one to be used with a client, and eventually by the client.' (page 16)

What are the values which sanction the mandate for work?
'When the worker's own purposes are used to sanction the work, it is the values on which the intervention is founded which succeed or fail in confirming that mandate.' (page 17)

Chapter 3 – Exploring Problems

Have the problems been properly scanned, was in-depth discussion avoided in the early stages?
'The intention is to get all of the problems out in the open, and in brief form, so that the range of difficulties can be seen.' (page 27)

Are the agreed priorities genuinely related to the client's priorities or to a statutory process?

'If a mandated problem exists it must be the first priority . . . The other priorities are the client's own, derived after discussion with the worker.' (pages 30–31)

Are the problems specified in a clear and unambiguous way, are the problem statements written in the client's own words, perhaps beginning with 'I . . .' or 'We . . .'?
'Questions that cover behaviour and questions that establish detail are to be encouraged at this stage and professional jargon is to be avoided.' (pages 32–33)

Chapter 4 – The Written Agreement

Has the client made clear the connection between the goal and the selected problem, and is the goal as clear as possible?
'A clear specific statement of the problem will help to point to a clear, specific statement of the goal.' (page 48)

How far is the goal within the client's power to achieve within the time limit?
'If the goal concerns changes in another person's behaviour, control over a successful outcome is removed from clients, except to the extent that they can influence that behaviour; in short, to what extent will changes in the client's own behaviour affect the behaviour of somebody else? . . . efforts increase as we approach a deadline, and this natural effect is harnessed by task-centred practice.' (pages 49 and 52)

Is the goal desirable and is the client motivated to achieve it?
'In task-centred practice underlying motives are explored only to help the client check them in relation to the explicit goal, and to reinforce the desirability of the goal . . . The goal should be as clear as possible, within the capacity of the client to achieve and ethically acceptable to the practitioner.' (pages 50 and 51)

Chapter 5 – Tasks

Are the tasks a series of steps, are they being developed as part of an overall plan?
'seen and planned as a linked series of events which cumulatively lead to the agreed goal.' (page 61)

Has there been joint development of tasks with a recognition that clients bring expertise to the work?
'even in situations of maximum support it is vital to hold firmly on to the principle that the client has some expertise to bring to the work.' (page 67)

Has the Task Implementation Sequence been used?
'After the task has been formulated in general terms and agreed to by the client, workers should:

- enhance commitment
- plan task implementation
- analyse obstacles
- model, rehearse and use guided practice
- summarize.' (pages 68–70)

Chapter 6 – Ending the Work

Has the review of the work included the seven guideline questions?
1 Is the Selected Problem the one which you most wanted help with?
2 If not, what is the problem which you would have liked help with?
3 How much of the original goal do you think has been achieved?
4 How much of the original goal do other people think you have achieved?
5 What do you think about this way of working?
6 How do you feel about coping in the future now that the Agreement has ended?
7 Is any follow-up agreed? If so, why? (pages 81–86)

Are short-term agreements to be used within long-term involvement?
'Intervention can be considered as the period of the agreement, running through from problem to goal via tasks. Maintenance is the work undertaken on a regular basis to provide a consistent and relatively unchanged service.' (page 86–87)

Is the agency supportive of task-centred work?
'task-centred socal work is a relatively intense burst of work in a brief period' of time . . . An agency whose work patterns are typically long and thin . . . might find it difficult to support task-centred interventions.' (page 90)

Appendix 2   A Guide to the Task-Centred Literature

This guide is a selective list of books and articles specifically concerned with task-centred practice. The literature is arranged under different categories for ease of access; inevitably some references fall in more than one category, but we have tried to keep duplication to a minimum.

With grateful thanks to Anne E. Fortune, editor U.S. *Task-centred Newsletter*.

Communication

Epstein, L., (1985), *Talking and Listening: A Guide to the Helping Interview*, Columbus, Ohio: C. E. Merrill.

Fortune, A. E., (1979a), 'Communication in task-centred treatment', *Social Work*, 24, September, pp. 390–6.

Fortune, A. E. (1981), 'Communication processes in social work practice', *Social Service Review*, 55, 1, pp. 93–128.

Developing contracts and tasks

Fortune, A. E. (1985b), 'Planning duration and termination of treatment', *Social Service Review*, 59, 1, pp. 647–62.

Rooney, R. H. (1988b), 'Socialization strategies for involuntary clients', *Social Casework*, 69, March, pp. 131–40.

Sucato, V. (1978), 'The problem-solving process in short-term and long-term service', *Social Service Review*, 52, June, pp. 244–64.

Hepworth, D. H. (1979), 'Early removal of resistance in task-centred casework', *Social Work*, 26, July, pp. 317–22.

Reid, W. J. (1975), 'A test of a task-centred approach', *Social Work*, 20, January, pp. 3–9.

Reid, W. J. (1987b), 'The family problem-solving sequence', *Family Therapy*, 14, 2, pp. 135–46.

Reid, W. J. (in press), *Task Strategies: An Empirical Approach to Clinical Social Work*, New York: Columbia University Press.

Evaluation and research

Benbenishty, R. (1989), 'Combining the single-system and group approaches to evaluate treatment effectiveness on the agency level', *Journal of Social Service Research*, **12**, 3/4, pp. 31–48.

Benbenishty, R. and Ben-Zaken, A. (1988), 'Computer-aided process of monitoring task-centred family interventions', *Social Work Research and Abstracts*, **24**, Spring, pp. 7–9.

Blizinsky, M. and Reid, W. (1980), 'Problem focus and outcome in brief treatment', *Social Work*, **25**, March, pp. 89–98.

Davis, I. P. and Reid, W. J. (1988), 'Event analysis in clinical practice and process research', *Social Casework*, **69**, May, pp. 298–307.

Epstein, L., Tolson, E. R. and Reid, W. J., (1978), 'Dissemination', in *The Task-Centred System*, edited by William J. Reid, New York: Columbia University Press.

Garvin, C. (1986), 'Development research for task-centred group work with chronic mental patients', *Social Work with Groups*, **9**, Fall, pp. 31–42.

Gibbons, J. S., Bow, I., Butler, J. and Powell, J. (1979), 'Clients' reactions to task-centred casework: a follow-up study', *British Journal of Social Work*, **9**, 2, pp. 203–15.

Goldberg, E. M., Gibbons, J. and Sinclair, I. (1984), *Problems, Tasks and Outcomes: The Evaluation of Task-Centred Casework in Three Settings*, National Institute Social Services Library, No. 47, London: Allen and Unwin.

Kanter, J. S. (1983), 'Clinical application of task-centred social work practice', *Clinical Social Work Journal*, **11**, 3, pp. 228–44.

Reid, W. J. (1987a), 'Evaluating an intervention in developmental research, *Journal of Social Service Research*, **11**, 1, pp. 17–37.

Rooney, R. H. (1988a), 'Measuring task-centred training effects on practice: results of an audiotape study in a public agency', *Journal of Continuing Social Work Education*, **4**, 4, pp. 2–7.

Wodarski, J. S., Saffir, M. and Frazer, M. (1982), 'Using research to evaluate the effectiveness of task-centred casework', *Journal of Applied Social Sciences*, **7**, Spring, pp. 70–82.

Foster care and adoption

Rooney, R. H. (1981), 'A task-centred reunification model for foster care', in *The Challenge of Partnership: Working with Parents of Children in Foster Care*, edited by Anthony N. Maluccio and Paula A. Sinanoglu, New York: Child Welfare League of America.

Rzepnicki, T. L. (1985), 'Task-centred intervention in Foster Care Services: Working with Families Who Have Children in Placement', in *Task-Centred Practice with Families and Groups*, edited by Anne E. Fortune, New York: Springer Publishing Company.

Williams, S. and Cunningham, A. (1984), 'Rehabilitation and risk', *Adoption and Fostering*, **8**, 2, pp. 17–22.

Groupwork

Fortune, A. E. (1985a), 'Treatment Groups', in *Task-Centred Practice with Families and Groups*, edited by Anne E. Fortune, New York: Springer Publishing Company.

Garvin, C. (1974), 'Task-centred group work', *Social Service Review*, **48**, December, pp. 494–507.

Garvin, C. (1985), 'Practice with Task-centred Groups', in *Task-centred Practice with Families and Groups*, edited by Anne E. Fortune, New York: Springer Publishing Company.
Garvin, C. D., Reid, W. J. and Epstein, L (1976), 'A task-centred approach', in *Theories of Social Work with Groups*, edited by Robert W. Roberts and Helen Northen, New York: Columbia University Press.

Homelessness

Fellin, P. and Brown, K. S. (1989), 'Application of homelessness to teaching social work foundation content', *Journal of Teaching in Social Work*, 3, 1, pp. 17–33.
Phillips, M. H., DeChillo, N., Kronenfeld, D. and Middleton-Jeter, V. (1988), 'Homeless families: services made a difference', *Social Casework*, 69, January, pp. 48–53.

Juvenile justice and adolescents

Bass, M. (1977), 'Toward a model of treatment for runaway girls in detention,' in *Task-Centred Practice*, edited by William J. Reid and Laura Epstein, New York: Columbia Press.
Garvin, C. (1977), 'Strategies for group work with adolescents', in *Task-Centred Practice*, edited by William J. Reid and Laura Epstein, New York: Columbia University Press.
Larsen, J. and Mitchell, C. T. (1980), 'Task-centred strength-oriented group work with delinquents', *Social Casework*, 61, March, pp. 154–63.
Rooney, R. H. (1977), 'Adolescent groups in public schools,' in *Task-Centred Practice*. Edited by William J. Reid and Laura Epstein, New York: Columbia University Press.

Management

Rooney, R. H. and Wanless, M. (1985), 'A Model for Caseload Management Based on Task-centred Practice', in *Task-Centred Practice with Families and Groups*, edited by Anne E. Fortune, New York: Springer Publishing Company.
Parihar, B. (1984), *Task-centred Management in Human Services*, Springfield, Illinois: Charles C. Thomas.
Parihar, B. (1985), 'Problem-Oriented Management: An Administrative Practice Model', in *Task-Centred Practice with Families and Groups*, edited by Anne E. Fortune, New York: Springer Publishing Company.

Mental health

Brown, L. B. (1977), 'Treating problems of psychiatric patients', in *Task-Centred Practice*, edited by William J. Reid and Laura Epstein, New York: Columbia University Press.
Gibbons, J., Bow, I. and Butler, J. (1984), 'Task-centred Work after Parasuicide', in *Problems, Tasks and Outcomes: The Evaluation of Task-Centred Casework in Three Settings*, edited by E. M. Goldberg, J. Gibbons, and I. Sinclair, National Institute Social Services Library, No. 47, London: Allen and Unwin.
Newcome, K. (1985), 'Task-centred Group Work with the Chronically Mentally Ill

in Day Treatment', in *Task-Centred Practice with Families and Groups*, edited by Anne E. Fortune, New York: Springer Publishing Company.

Multi-cultural practice

Nofz, M. P. (1988), 'Alcohol abuse and culturally marginal American Indians: a task-centred approach', *Social Casework*, **69**, 2, February, pp. 67–73.

Probation

Dobson, G. (1979), 'Towards task-centred casework: the differential treatment unit 1972–78'. From J. F. S. King (ed), *Pressures and Change in the Probation Service*, Papers presented to the 11th Cropwood Round Table Conference, December 1978. Cropwood Conference Series No. 11, University of Cambridge.
Goldberg, E. M. and Stanley, S. J. (1979), 'A task-centred approach to probation'. From J. F. S. King (ed), *Pressures and Change in the Probation Service*, Papers presented to the 11th Cropwood Round Table Conference, December 1978. Cropwood Conference Series No. 11, University of Cambridge.
Goldberg, E. M., Stanley, S. J. with Kenrick, J. (1984), 'Task-centred casework in a probation setting', in *Problems, Tasks and Outcomes: The Evaluation of Task-Centred Casework in Three Settings*, edited by E. M. Goldberg, J. Gibbons, and I. Sinclair, National Institute Social Services Library, No. 47, London: Allen and Unwin.
Marshall, P. (1977), 'Task centred practice in a probation setting', in *Practising Social Work*, edited by Robert Harris, University of Leicester, School of Social Work.

School settings

Epstein, L (1977), 'A project in school social work', in *Task-Centred Practice*, edited by William J. Reid and Laura Epstein, New York: Columbia University Press.
Reid, W. J., Epstein, L., Brown, L., Tolson, E. and Rooney, R. H. (1980), 'Task-centred school social work', *Social Work in Education*, **2**, January, pp. 7–24.

Training and student supervision

Basso, R. (1987), 'Teacher and student problem solving activities in educational supervisory session, *Journal of Social Work Education*, **23**, 3, Fall, pp. 67–73.
Fortune, A. E. and Rathbone-McCuan, E. (1981), 'Education in gerontological social work: application of the task-centred model', *Journal of Education for Social Work*, **17**, Fall, pp. 98–105.
Larsen, J. A. (1980), 'Competency-based and task-centred practicum instruction', *Journal of Education for Social Work*, **16**, 1, pp. 87–94.
McCaughen, N. and Vickery, A. (1982), 'Staging the play,' *Social Work Today*, **14**, 2, pp. 11–13.
Moffatt, R. (1977), 'Using the task centred model as an introduction to casework, in student supervision', *Contemporary Social Work Education*, **1**, 1, pp. 24–37.
Reid, W. J., and Beard, C. (1980), 'An evaluation of in-service training in a public welfare setting', *Administration in Social Work*, 4, Spring, pp. 71–85.
Rooney, R. H. (1985), 'Does inservice training make a difference? Results of a

pilot study of task-centred dissemination in a public social service setting', *Journal of Social Service Research*, 8, 3, pp. 33–50.

Rooney, R. H. (1988a), 'Measuring task-centred training effects on practice: results of an audiotape study in a public agency', *Journal of Continuing Social Work Education*, 4, 4, pp. 2–7.

Tolson, E. R. (1985), 'Teaching and Measuring Task-centred Skills: The Skill Assessment Teaching Model', in *Task-Centred Practice with Families and Groups*, edited by Anne E. Fortune, New York: Springer Publising Company.

Work with children, families and couples

Benbenishty, R. (1988), 'Assessment of task-centred interventions with families in Israel', *Journal of Social Service Research*, 11, 4, pp. 19–43.

Butler, J., Bow, I. and Gibbons, J. (1978), 'Task-centred casework with marital problems', *British Journal of Social Work*, 8, Summer, pp. 393–409.

Dahms, W. R. (1977), 'A task-centred approach to treatment planning', *Child Care Quarterly*, 6, Fall, pp. 196–203.

Fortune, A. E. (1979b), 'Problem-solvig process in task-centred treatment with adults and children', *Journal of Social Service Research*, 2, Summer, pp. 357–71.

Fortune, A. E. (1985c), 'Families and Family Treatment', in *Task-Centred Practice with Families and Groups*, edited by Anne E. Fortune, New York: Springer Publishing Company.

Reid, W. J. (1981), 'Family treatment within a task-centred framework, in *Models of Family Treatment*, edited by Eleanor Reardon Tolson and William J. Reid, New York: Columbia University Press.

Reid, W. J. (1985a), *Family Problem Solving*, New York: Columbia University Press.

Reid, W. J. (1985b), 'Work with Families', in *Task-Centred Practice with Families and Groups*, edited by Anne E. Fortune, New York: Springer Publishing Company.

Reid, W. J. and Helmer, K. (1985), *Session Tasks in Family Treatment*, State University of New York at Albany, School of Social Welfare.

Tolson, E. R. (1977), 'Alleviating marital communication problems', in *Task-Centred Practice*, edited by William J. Reid and Laura Epstein, New York: Columbia University Press.

Work with older people

Cormican, E. (1977), 'Task-centred model for work with the aged', *Social Casework*, 58, October, pp. 490–494.

Dierking, B., Brown, M. and Fortune, A. E. (1980), 'Task-centred treatment in a residential facility for the elderly: a clinical trial', *Journal of Gerontological Social Work*, 2, Spring, pp. 225–40.

Rathbone-McCuan, E. (1985), 'Intergenerational Family Practice with Older Families', in *Task-Centred Practice with Families and Groups*, edited by Anne E. Fortune, New York: Springer Publishing Company.

Scharlach, A. E. (1985), 'Social group work with institutionalized elders: a task-centred approach', *Social Work with Groups*, 8, Fall, pp. 33–47.

Toseland, R. W. and Coppola, M. (1985), 'A Task-centred Approach to Group Work with Older Persons', in *Task-Centred Practice with Families and Groups*, edited by Anne E. Fortune, New York: Springer Publishing Company.

References

Benbenishty, R. (1989), 'Combining the single-system and group approaches to evaluate treatment effectiveness on the agency level', *Journal of Social Service Research*, **12**, 3/4, pp. 31–48.

Blizinsky, M. and Reid, W. (1980), 'Problem focus and outcome in brief treatment', *Social Work*, **25**, March, pp. 89–98.

Booth, T. (1983), 'Residents' Views, Rights and Institutional Care', in *Speaking of Clients*, edited by M. Fisher, Sheffield: University of Sheffield, Joint Unit for Social Services Research.

Bottoms, A. E. and McWilliams, W. (1979), 'A Non-treatment Paradigm for Probation', *British Journal of Social Work*, **9**, pp. 159–202.

Brewer, C. and Lait, J. (1980), *Can Social Work Survive?* London: Temple Smith.

British Association of Social Workers (1980), *Clients are Fellow Citizens Report of the Working Party on Client Participation in Social Work*, Birmingham: BASW.

Butler, J., Bow, I. and Gibbons, J. (1978), 'Task-centred casework with marital problems', *British Journal of Social Work*, **8**, Summer, pp. 393–409.

Corden, J. and Preston-Shoot, M. (1987), 'Contract or con trick? A reply to Rojek and Collins', *British Journal of Social Work*, **17**, 5, pp. 535–44.

Coulshed, V. (1988), *Social Work Practice*, London: Macmillan.

Davies, M. (1981), *The Essential Social Worker*, London: Heinemann.

Davis, I. P. and Reid, W. J. (1988), 'Event analysis in clinical practice and process research', *Social Casework*, **69**, May, pp. 298–307.

Day, P. (1981), *Social Work and Social Control*, London: Tavistock.

DHSS (1983), *Personal Social Services – Disclosure of Information to Clients*, LAC (83), 14.

de Shazer, S. (1985), *Keys to Solution in Brief Therapy*, New York: W. W. Norton.

Devore, W. and Schlesinger, E. G. (1981), *Ethnic-sensitive Social Work Practice*, St. Louis, USA: C.V. Mosby Company.

Doel, M., (1989), 'A Practice Curriculum to Promote Accelerated Learning', in *Towards a Practice-led Curriculum*, edited by J. Phillipson, M. Richards, and D. Sawder, London: National Institute for Social Work.

Doel, M. and Lawson, B. (1986), 'Open records: the client's right to partnership', *British Journal of Social Work*, **16**, 4, pp. 407–30.

Doel, M. and Lawson, B. (1989a), 'A paper dialogue', *Community Care*, No. 761, pp. 26–7.

Doel, M. and Lawson, B. (1989b), *A Paper Dialogue*, Sheffield: University of Sheffield, Joint Unit for Social Services Research (video, 48 minutes).

Epstein, L. (1985), *Talking and Listening: A Guide to the Helping Interview*, Columbus, Ohio: C. E. Merrill.

Epstein, L. (1988), *Helping People: The Task-Centred Approach*, second edition, Columbus, Ohio: C. E. Merrill.

Fischer, J. (1973), 'Is Casework Effective: A Review', *Social Work*, January, pp. 5–20.

Fischer, J. (1978), 'Does Anything Work?', *Journal of Social Services Research*, 1, 3, pp. 215–34.

Fisher, M. (1983), 'The Meaning of Client Satisfaction', in *Speaking of Clients*, edited by M. Fisher, Sheffield: University of Sheffield, Joint Unit for Social Services Research.

Fisher, M. (1990), *Partnership Practice with Clients with Dementia*, Sheffield: Universities of Bradford and Sheffield (unpublished research paper from Social Work in Partnership Programme).

Fisher, M., Marsh, P. and Phillips, D. (1986), *In and Out of Care*, London: Batsford.

Fisher, R. and Ury, W. (1982), *Getting to Yes*, London: Hutchinson.

Fortune, A. E. (1981), 'Communication processes in social work practice', *Social Service Review*, 55, 1, pp. 93–128.

Fortune, A. E. (ed.) (1985a), *Task-Centred Practice with Families and Groups*, New York: Springer Publishing.

Fortune, A. E. (1985b), 'Planning duration and termination of treatment', *Social Service Review*, 59, 1, pp. 647–62.

Garvin, C. (1974), 'Task-centred group work', *Social Service Review*, 48, December, pp. 494–507.

Gibbons, J. S., Bow, I., Butler, J. and Powell, J. (1979), 'Clients' reactions to task-centred casework: a follow-up study', *British Journal of Social Work*, 9, 2, pp. 203–15.

Goldberg, E. M., Gibbons, J. and Sinclair, I., (1984), *Problems, Tasks and Outcomes: The Evaluation of Task-Centred Casework in Three Settings*, National Institute Social Services Library, No. 47, London: Allen and Unwin.

Goldberg, E. M., Walker, D. and Robinson, J. (1977), 'Exploring the task-centred casework method', *Social Work Today*, 9, 2, pp. 9–14.

Goldstein, A. (1973),*Structured Learning Therapy*, New York: Academic Press.

Gorrell-Barnes, G. (1984), *Working with Families*, London: Macmillan.

Grey, A. L. and Dermody, H. E. (1972), 'Reports of Casework Failure', *Social Casework*, November, pp. 535–43.

Hari, V. (1977), 'Instituting Short-term Casework in a "Long-term" Agency', in *Task-centred practice*, edited by William J. Reid and Laura Epstein, New York: Columbia University Press.

Heap, K. (1985), *The Practice of Social Work with Groups*, London: George Allen and Unwin.

Hepworth, D. H. (1979), 'Early removal of resistance in task-centred casework', *Social Work*, 26, July, pp. 317–22.

International Federation of Social Workers (1976), *International Code of Ethics*, Vienna: IFSW.

Ivanoff, A., Blythe, B. and Briar, S. (1987), 'The Empirical Clinical practice Debate', *Social Casework*, 69, May, pp. 290–8.

Laing, R. D. and Esterson, A. (1964), *Sanity, Madness and the Family*, London: Tavistock Publications.

Larsen, J. and Mitchell, C. T. (1980), 'Task-centred strength-oriented group work with delinquents', *Social Casework*, **61**, March, pp. 154–63.

Maluccio, A. N. (1979), *Learning from Clients*, New York: The Free Press.

Marsh, P. (1983), 'Researching Practice and Practising Research in Child Care Social Work', in *Speaking of Clients*, edited by M. Fisher, Sheffield: University of Sheffield, Joint Unit for Social Services Research.

Marsh, P. (1986), 'Natural Families and Children in Care: an agenda for practice development', *Adoption and Fostering*, **10**, pp. 20–5.

Marsh, P. (1990), 'Changing Practice in Child Care – the Children Act 1989', *Adoption and Fostering*, **14**, pp. 27–30.

Marshall, P. (1987), 'Task centred practice in a probation setting', in *Practising Social Work*, edited by Robert Harris, University of Leicester, School of Social Work.

Mayer, J. E. and Timms, N. (1970), *The Client Speaks*, London: Routledge and Kegan Paul.

National Council of Voluntary Organizations (1984), *Clients' Rights – Report of a working party established by the N.C.V.O.*, London: Bedford Square Press.

National Institute for Social Work (1988) *A Positive Choice – Report of the Independent Review of Residential Care*, London: Her Majesty's Stationery Office.

Nofz, M. P. (1988), 'Alcohol abuse and culturally marginal American Indians: a task-centred approach, *Social Casework*, **69**, 2, February, pp. 67–73.

O'Connor, R. and Reid, W. J. (1986), Dissatisfaction with Brief Treatment, *Social Service Review*, December, pp. 526–37.

Ovretveit, J. (1986), *Improving Social Work Records and Practice*, Birmingham: BASW Publications.

Pincus, A. and Minahan, A. (1973), *Social Work Practice: Model and Method*, Itasca, Illinois: F. E. Peacock.

Pincus, L. and Dare, C. (1978), *Secrets in the Family*, London: Faber and Faber.

Priestley, P. et al (1978), *Social Skills and Personal Problem Solving – A Handbook of Methods*, London: Tavistock.

Reid,W. J. (1963), *An Experimental Study of the Methods Used in Casework Treatment*, New York: Columbia University Doctoral Dissertation.

Reid, W. J. (1975), 'A test of task-centred approach,' *Social Work*, **20**, January, 3–9.

Reid, W. J. (1978), *The Task-Centred System*, New York: Columbia University Press.

Reid, W. J. (1985), *Family Problem Solving*, New York: Columbia University Press.

Reid, W. J. (1987a), 'Evaluating an intervention in developmental research', *Journal of Social Service Research*, **11**, 1, pp. 17–37.

Reid, W. J. (1987b), 'The family problem-solving sequence', *Family Therapy*, **14**, 2, pp. 135–46.

Reid, W. J. (in press), *Task Strategies: An Empirical Approach to Clinical Social Work*, New York: Columbia University Press.

Reid, W. J. and Epstein, L. (1972), *Task-Centred Casework*, New York: Columbia University Press.

Reid, W. J. and Hanrahan, P. (1981), 'The Effectiveness of Social Work: Recent Evidence', in *Evaluative Research in Social Care*, edited by E. M. Goldberg, and N. Connelly, London: Heinemann Education Books.

Reid, W. J. and Hanrahan, P. (1982), 'Recent Evaluations of Social Work: Grounds for Optimism', *Social Work*, July, pp. 328–40.

Reid, W. J. and Helmer, K. (1985), *Session Tasks in Family Treatment*, State University of New York at Albany, School of Social Welfare.

Reid, W. J. and Shyne, A. W. (1969), *Brief and Extended Casework*, New York: Columbia University Press.

Rhodes, M. L. (1986), *Ethical Dilemmas in Social Work Practice*, London: Routledge and Kegan Paul.

Rojek, C. and Collins, S. A. (1987), 'Contract or con trick?', *British Journal of Social Work*, 17, 2, pp. 199–212.

Rooney, R. H. (1988a), 'Measuring task-centred training effects on practice: results of an audiotape study in a public agency', *Journal of Continuing Social Work Education*, 4, 4, pp. 2–7.

Rooney, R. H. (1988b), 'Socialization strategies for involuntary clients', *Social Casework*, 69, March, pp. 131–40.

Sainsbury, E. (1983), 'Client Studies and Social Policy', in *Speaking of Clients*, edited by M. Fisher, Sheffield: University of Sheffield, Joint Unit for Social Services Research.

Sainsbury, E. (1989), *'What clients value'*. Unpublished paper given to BASW Study Day of Task-Centred Practice Special Interest Group, April.

Sainsbury, E., Nixon, S. and Phillips, D. (1982), *Social Work in Focus*, London: Routledge and Kegan Paul.

Seligman, M. E. P. (1975), *Helplessness*, San Francisco: Freeman.

Shaw, I. F. (1984), 'Literature Review. Consumer Evaluations of the Personal Social Services', *British Journal of Social Work*, 14, pp. 277–84.

Sheldon, B. (1986), 'Social Work Effectiveness Experiments: Review and Implications', *British Journal of Social Work*, 16, pp. 223–41.

Stevenson, O. and Parsloe, P. (1978), *Social Service Teams: The Practitioner's View*, London: Her Majesty's Stationery Office.

Thomlison, R. J. (1984), 'Something Works: evidence from Practice Effectiveness Studies', *Social Work*, Jan-Feb, pp. 51–6.

Thorpe, D. et al. (1980), *In and Out of Care*, London: George Allen and Unwin.

Watson, D. (ed.) (1985), A Code of Ethics for Social Work – The Second Step, London: Routledge and Kegan Paul.

Wodarski, J. S., Saffir, M. and Frazer, M. (1982), 'Using research to evaluate the effectiveness of task-centred casework', *Journal of Applied Social Sciences*, 7, Spring, pp. 70–82.

Wood, K. M. (1978), 'Casework Effectivness: A New Look at the Research Evidence', *Social Work*, November, pp. 437–58.

Index

Name Index

The Police and Social Workers

Second Edition

Terry Thomas

Social workers and police officers are in daily contact with one another in various areas of their work. This book offers a clear guide to that inter-agency work and critically examines how it is carried out in practice.

This second edition of the book has been substantially revised to take account of changes in the law, policy and procedures affecting both police and social workers. In particular the Children Act 1989, The Criminal Justice Act 1991 and the findings of the Royal Commission on Criminal Justice 1993. The opportunity has also been taken to revise parts of the original text to ensure as clear a light as possible is thrown on police-social work collaboration – illustrating both the positive and the negative.

Terry Thomas is Senior Lecturer in Social Work at Leeds Metropolitan University.

1994   346 pages   1 85742 157 4   £14.95

Price subject to change without notification

THE essential SOCIAL WORKER

An introduction to professional practice in the 1990s

THIRD EDITION

MARTIN DAVIES

This third edition has been radically revised and updated and contains an entirely new chapter providing a clear outline of the historical and policy-related framework within which social work operates in areas of particular practice - child care, disability, mental health, old age and criminal justice.

The Essential Social Worker defends the idea of a broadly based profession seeking to maintain disadvantaged people in the community. It bravely confronts the shallowness of many short-term fashions and argues that social work is a uniquely humane contributor to the achievement of welfare in the 1990s and beyond.

A careful reading will ensure that the student gains an understanding of the role of social work in a complex urban society and develops an awareness of the debates which surround it. Social work is often subject to public criticism, but, as the author shows, it has continued to grow in scale and in influence throughout the 20th century, and, although its structure will continue to evolve, social work will remain essential in any society which regards itself as democratic and humane.

Martin Davies is Executive Director of the School of Social Work, University of East Anglia

1994   240 pages   Hbk   1 85742 100 0   £29.95
                     Pbk   1 85742 101 9   £12.95

Personal Safety for Social Workers

Commissioned by
The Suzy Lamplugh Trust

Pauline Bibby

Foreword by
Diana Lamplugh OBE

This book is aimed at employers, managers and staff in social work agencies.

In part 1, *Personal Safety for Social Workers* deals with the respective roles and responsibilities of employers and employees are discussed, and offers guidance on developing a workplace personal safety policy. The design and management of the workplace are considered and guidelines provided for social workers working away from the normal work base. Part 2 contains detailed guidelines for use by individual social workers in a variety of work situations. Part 3 addresses training issues and provides a number of sample training programmes.

The message of this book is that proper attention to risk can reduce both the incidence of aggression and its development into violent acts.

1994   224 pages   1 85742 195 7   £16.95

Advocacy Skills

A HANDBOOK FOR HUMAN SERVICE PROFESSIONALS

Neil Bateman

Advocacy is a skill used by many people in human service organisations. Social workers, community medical staff and advice workers are a few who will use such skills. Advocacy is used to overcome obstacles and to secure tangible results for customers – extra money, better services and housing. Neil Bateman's book sets out a model for effective professional practice, and outlines a number of approaches to advocacy.

This is a seminal work; no other book has been published in the UK which explains how advocacy skills can be used and developed. Advocacy is becoming part of the everyday work of many people. Advocacy Skills will be a valuable handbook for anyone concerned with the rights of others.

Neil Bateman is currently a Principal Officer with Suffolk County Council, an adviser to the Association of County Councils and a visiting lecturer at the University of East Anglia.

1995   176 pages   1 85742 200 7   £14.95

WORKING TOGETHER IN
Child Protection
An exploration of the multi-disciplinary task and system
MICHAEL MURPHY

This book is a resource for all practitioners, students, managers and trainers who work in the child protection field. It explores the detailed working arrangements of one child protection system and examines the roles and perspectives of the agencies and practitioners who make up that system. It uses examples that are drawn from current practice to outline crucial arguments in the text. It suggests that multi-disciplinary child protection work is both complex and difficult, claiming that a series of structural blockages exist to effective joint working, in particular that we all harbour an ignorance of the perspective and reality of the other agencies and practitioners within the system.

The work goes on to propose a number of measures to be taken by practitioner, agency and government departments that will promote multi-disciplinary working at all levels, suggesting that good multi-disciplinary communication, co-operation and action is synonymous with good child protection work.

The child protection system in England and Wales is used as a case study, but comparisons are drawn with child protection systems in other parts of the world. It is argued that the key concepts and conventions of effective multi-disciplinary child protection work are constant and go beyond the boundaries of single systems.

Michael Murphy is co-ordinator on a Multi-disciplinary Child Protection Resource project.

1995   224 pages   Hbk   1 85742 197 3   £35.00
Pbk   1 85742 198 1   £14.95

Contested Adoptions

Research, law, policy and practice

**Edited by
Murray Ryburn**

This is the first book to consider the law and research and its application in relation to contested adoption proceedings.. It examines issues of policy and practice including such matters as attachment, separation and assessment, and the role of the guardian ad litem. It locates contested adoptions within the wider framework of the Children Act 1989 and, perhaps most importantly, it includes contribution from those with personal experience of contested adoptions. It is a book which will be invaluable to all those who work in the adoption field, including social work practitioners, guardians ad litem, and barristers and solicitors practising family law, as well as social work students and teachers on DipSW courses.

Murray Ryburn is Director of Social Work Courses at the University of Birmingham.

1994   232 pages   Hbk   1 85742 187 6   £32.00
         Pbk   1 85742 188 4   £16.95